The Space Available Bible

ALSO BY MARCUS SEITZ

Hiking the Appalachian Trail - A Couple's Journey through America's Wilderness

Coronavirus - Race for the Cure

The Space Available Bible

Traveling the World for Free on Military Aircraft

MARCUS SEITZ

Cover photo by Pixabay

Dedication

The adventurous spirit of past, current and future Space-A travelers that continually circumnavigate the globe utilizing this tremendous resource to help quench their wanderlust.

Preface

Back in the late 1980s, my friend Jeff and I attended different universities in Washington State. We were both enrolled as cadets in the U.S. Army Reserve Officer Training Corps (ROTC) programs at our respective institutions. During spring break in our junior year, Jeff asked if I wanted to visit his parents who were currently stationed at Schofield Barracks in Hawaii. Given the dismal weather in Washington during March where I hadn't seen the sun in the past three months, I happily agreed despite having no funds for such an adventure. Luckily for me, Jeff knew about Space Available (Space-A) travel with the military. He told me that the military had planes flying around the world constantly, and if there were extra spaces available on any aircraft, they would sometimes let eligible people catch a ride (or hop). Jeff informed me that cadets were eligible, and sure enough, we managed to hop on an Air Force plane flying from McChord Air Force Base, in Tacoma, Washington to Travis Air Force Base in California, with follow-on service to Hickam Air Force Base in Honolulu, Hawaii. Given how easy it was to catch a flight to Hawaii at no cost, I wondered why more people didn't take advantage of this great benefit. Well, I soon discovered why when I attempted to return to the mainland.

This book is designed to provide a comprehensive guide to military Space-A air travel. It contains an abundance of references and should answer most any question you may have concerning flying Space-A. It is a great benefit for eligible personnel, but it is important to understand the drawbacks so you make the best use of this means of transport. After reading this book, you will become expert in utilizing this benefit, and I hope you are soon traveling all over the world at very minimal cost.

Acknowledgments

To the dedicated travel bloggers and website curators that both espouse the glories and challenges of Space-A travel in their many forums. Also, the plethora of resources and services provided by the Air Mobility Command.

Introduction

Space-A is an abbreviation for Space Available air transportation on government-owned or controlled aircraft. Sometimes seats are made available on these aircraft for eligible passengers, depending on the aircraft's mission and cargo allowances. If you have patience and flexibility, this benefit may allow you to travel the world at little or no cost. Space-A travel is not available to everyone. The general rule of thumb is that service members associated with the Department of Defense, including dependents, and some civilian DoD employees may be eligible for Space-A travel. Additional eligibility is discussed later in the book.

Space-A travel combines frugality with adventure but sometimes, just like a box of chocolates, you don't know what you are going to get. There is no guarantee that you will be able to take a flight; reservations are not accepted. The Department of Defense (DoD) has limited obligations towards travelers using Space-A; there are no guarantees during different flight segments or for return flights. Space-A passengers may be removed from flights if circumstances change like an altered mission, equipment failure, or not enough flight personnel. Thus, it is recommended that travelers have sufficient resources to address the possible need for commercial transportation, lodging, and other expenses if Space-A plans alter. You will not be reimbursed for any associated expenses related to flying Space-A. Space-A travel may not be used for personal gain, in connection with a business enterprise, or for employment.

Space-A travel also may not be used when international or theater restrictions prohibit such travel. For instance, once my wife was deployed to Kuwait. I looked into flights going to Kuwait, but that route was restricted. Flights going to Guantanamo Bay, Cuba, are limited to certain personnel. Although I must say that once, as a Space-A passenger, I was allowed on a flight that made a short stop in Guantanamo, but with a final destination elsewhere. During our stop, we were restricted to a specific room on base while the plane was prepped to continue to Puerto Rico.

The organization that has responsibility for Space-A is the Air Mobility Command (AMC). AMC is a major command of the U.S. Air Force; it was created in 1992. It was formed from parts of Strategic Air Command (SAC) and the deactivated Military Airlift Command (MAC). You will sometimes still see references to MAC in older documents. AMC consists not only of active duty airmen but also includes the Air National Guard and Air Force Reserve; therefore, you might see Space-A flights originating or terminating at other than active duty bases. Civilian airliners and flight crews of the Civil Reserve Air Fleet also work with AMC. This means you may see Space-A flights at commercial airports like Sea-Tac (SEA) or Baltimore Washington (BWI).

The Space-A Process

The Space-A process consists of seven steps. They may seem overwhelming the first time you attempt to fly Space-A, but it does not take long to become an expert. After your first Space-A flight, you will understand both its benefits and its limitations. Space-A will truly open your window to the world, all at little or no cost. Remember that many travelers utilize Space-A almost every day, ranging from single passengers to large families with all their associated luggage. With some proper planning and understanding of the process, you will be able to start your own adventure. The steps are as follows:

- Determine Eligibility
- Find Your Category
- Plan Your Route
- Check Your Travel Documents
- Register
- Check-in
- Fly

Determine Eligibility

Space-A travel is not available to everyone. As there are many exceptions and specific requirements, it is difficult to outline a general eligibility rule. Perhaps the closest you can get would be to state that members of, or associated with the Department of Defense, including their dependents, may be eligible for Space-A travel. In order to determine if you are eligible examine *Table 3, Eligible Space Available Travelers, Priorities, and Approved Geographical Travel Segments* found in the *Department of Defense Instruction (DODI) 4515.13 Air Transportation Eligibility*. Its 70 pages may feel a bit mind-boggling, but the Space Available section is only 15 pages, and Table 3 is six pages.

Reading these instructions will give you a good general education in Space-A travel.

Find Category

As mentioned above, Table 3 in the *DODI 4515.13* provides a list of those people eligible to use Space-A travel. If you find that you are eligible, your next step is to determine what Space-A travel category you are. The categories are numerical, ranging from one to six. The lower your category number, the higher your priority. The order passengers are allowed on the plane is based on their category.

For example [see below], if a plane has three seats available for Space-A passengers but there are five eligible passengers in the terminal who want to get on the plane, only the travelers in the highest two categories will score seats for this particular flight.

Category I	1	Highest priority
Category III	2	Second highest priority
Category III	3	Third highest priority
Category IV	4	Fourth highest priority
Category V	5	Fifth highest priority
Category VI	6	Lowest priority (retired military)

Passenger A	Ralph	Category 1	*
Passenger B	Susan	Category 2	*
Passenger C	Paul	Category 2	*
Passenger D	Rick	Category 4	
Passenger E	Jean	Category 6	

In the example above, only passengers Ralph (A), Susan (B) and Paul (C) would be allowed on the plane. They rank the highest by category for the three available seats.

But, if in the example above, there were only two seats available for Space-A passengers on the plane, passenger Susan (B), and passenger Paul (C) who are both category 2, would be awarded a seat based on who registered for Space-A travel first. More on that later in the registration section.

Table 3 in *DODI 4515.13* lists 48 different situations where travelers may be eligible for Space-A travel. The entire table is available in the back of this book, but below is a partial listing of eligible individuals. While there are unique situations like special category residents (Cuban exiles for instance) who are eligible for Space-A travel only to and from Cuba, or American Samoa veterans residing in America Samoa, traveling to and from Hawaii for hospital care at a VA facility, most travelers will not fit these situations.

The majority of Space-A travelers will either be Category III (active duty on ordinary leave) or Category VI (reserves/national guard or retired military). Most dependents utilizing Space-A travel will fall under Category III.

Category I - Emergency Leave Unfunded Travel.

Transportation by the most expeditious routing only for bona fide immediate family emergencies, as determined by *DODI 1327.06* (Leave and Liberty Policy and Procedures) and Military Service regulations. This travel privilege will not be used in lieu of funded travel entitlements.

Emergency Travel in connection with serious illness, death, or impending death of a member of the immediate family of the following:

- United States citizen, DoD Civilian Employees stationed

overseas.

- Full-time, paid personnel of the American Red Cross serving with United States military services overseas.
- Uniformed service family members whose sponsors are stationed within the Continental United States (CONUS) and the emergency exists overseas.
- Family members of United States citizen civilian employees of the DoD when both sponsor and dependents are stationed overseas at the same location.

Category II - Accompanied Environmental and Morale Leave (EML).

- Sponsors on EML and accompanied family members.
- DoD Dependent School (DoDDS) teachers and their accompanied family members in EML status during school year holiday or vacation periods.

Category III - Ordinary Leave, Relatives, House Hunting Permissive Temporary Duty (TDY), Medal of Honor Holders, and Foreign Military.

- Members of the uniformed services in an ordinary or re-enlistment leave status.
- Military personnel traveling on permissive temporary duty (TDY) orders for house hunting.
- If the permissive TDY is for the purpose of a permanent change of station house hunting, the member travels in Category III and can be accompanied by one family member.
- Dependents of military members deployed for more than 365 consecutive days.
- Bona fide family members (up to age 23 with a valid identification card) of a service member of the uniformed

services when accompanied by their sponsor who is in an ordinary leave status within overseas areas between overseas stations and air terminals in the CONUS (Continental United States).

- This privilege does not apply to travel of dependents to or from a sponsor's restricted or unaccompanied tour location or to travel in a leave status to or from TDY locations. It applies only to round-trip travel to an overseas area or the CONUS with the sponsor. *DODI 4515.13* restricts the use of these privileges to establish a home for family members in an overseas area or the CONUS.
- Foreign exchange service members on permanent duty with the DoD, when in a leave status.

Category IV - Unaccompanied Environmental and Morale Leave (EML).

- Dependents where the military members are deployed for more than 30 consecutive days.
- Unaccompanied family members (18 years or older) traveling on EML orders. Family members under 18 must be accompanied by an adult family member who is traveling EML.
- DoDDS teachers or their family members (accompanied or unaccompanied) in an EML status during summer break.

Category V - Permissive TDY (Non-House Hunting), Students, Dependents, Post Deployment/Mobilization Respite Absence, and Others.

- Unaccompanied Command-sponsored dependents.
- Students whose sponsor is stationed in Alaska or Hawaii.
- Students enrolled in a trade school in the CONUS when the

> sponsor is stationed overseas.
>
> - Military personnel traveling on permissive TDY orders for other than house hunting.

Category VI – Retired, Dependents, Reserve, ROTC, Nuclear Propulsion Officer (NUPOC) and Civil Engineer Corps (CEC) members & 100% Disabled Vets.

- National Guard/Reserve Components/members of the Ready Reserve and members of the Standby Reserve who are on the Active Status List.
- Retired military members who are issued DD Form 2 and eligible to receive retired or retainer pay.
- Family members (with a valid identification card) of retired members when accompanied by a sponsor.
- As of August 13th, 2018, authorized veterans with a permanent service-connected disability rated as total or VA-100% Disabled Veteran.

Regarding the last bullet above, the primary regulation covering Space-A passenger transportation, *DODI 4515.13*, was updated on August 13, 2018. The National Defense Authorization Act for Fiscal Year 2019 introduced a policy change that provided eligibility for Veterans with a Permanent Service-connected Disability Rated as Total to compete for travel aboard Space-A passenger transportation, using surplus aircraft capacity.

These authorized veterans will be designated Space-A Travel Priority Category VI (6) with the authorization to travel in CONUS or directly between the CONUS and Alaska, Hawaii, Puerto Rico, the U.S. Virgin Islands, Guam, and American Samoa (Guam and American Samoa travelers may transit Hawaii or Alaska); or traveling within Alaska, Hawaii, Puerto Rico, or the U.S. Virgin Islands. Veterans with a permanent service-connected disability rated as total must have a DD Form 2765, "Department of Defense/Uniformed Services Identification and Privilege Card (tan-colored)." This an example of how the Space-A rules and regulations are constantly changing.

One feature not covered in the above categories is the approved geographical travel segments. But they are listed in Table 3 in the *DODI 4515.13*. The approved geographical travel segments list the origin and destination combinations as follows:

C-C	CONUS to CONUS
O-O	OCONUS to OCONUS
C-O	CONUS to OCONUS
O-C	OCONUS to CONUS

CONUS stands for Continental United States meaning the 48 contiguous states in the U.S. OCONUS stands for Outside the Continental United States meaning overseas including Hawaii and Alaska. The reason this is important is that you may find you are eligible based on a certain situation but then you could be limited in how you can use Space-A travel. For example, a particular Category I circumstance includes "unaccompanied dependents of members of the uniformed services who are assigned and domiciled in the CONUS." Travelers that are eligible under this situation can use Space-A travel from CONUS to OCONUS or OCONUS to CONUS but they are not allowed Space-A travel from CONUS to CONUS (domestic travel) or OCONUS to OCONUS.

If the process to determine your category and whether you can travel where you want to go is a bit confusing, do not worry. There are several options to help you determine whether you are eligible for Space-A travel and what your category is. You can simply contact any AMC terminal and they will help you with the eligibility determination and determining your correct category. You can also join several Facebook Space-A groups that have fellow Space-A travelers who are glad to help new Space-A travelers. More on that later.

Plan Route

After you have determined that you are eligible to use Space-A and you have found your category, it's time to plan your actual trip. There are Space-A flights throughout the entire world, including military and commercial airports in the U.S.; but they may not be exactly where you live, or where you want to start your journey. Your departure point may not always be the closest location to you; there are other factors to consider. The primary factors will be whether there are available flights, whether the flights have available seats, and most importantly, is the flight going where you want to travel? We live near Washington D.C., and the closest airport with Space-A flights is Andrews Air Force Base. Unfortunately, Andrews only has limited flights and most of them do not go to where I want to fly. Thus, I have to cast out a wider net and consider other places like Dover Air Force Base in Delaware, Baltimore-Washington International Airport in Baltimore, Joint Base McGuire-Dix-Lakehurst in New Jersey, or even Naval Station Norfolk in Southeast Virginia.

Another consideration is how you are going to get to the airport? You may be able to take public transportation which means you will not need to worry about parking. This is especially important when flying from a commercial airport as the parking fees can really accumulate. Most military facilities will have free long-term parking available, although the parking lots may be some distance from the terminal. Always ensure you register your vehicle when parking on military installations to avoid being towed. And from practical experience, ensure that all lights are off in your vehicle so your battery doesn't die before your return.

When deciding on your originating airport, make sure you research the flights that leave from that location. Most military airports will have a Facebook page that lists flight departures and arrivals up to 72 hours in advance. As part of your planning process, you can start to review airport Facebook pages before your trip to get an understanding of what type of flights leave from that airport. You can also call the terminal to ask about what type of flights normally leave from that particular location. Another possibility is to post a question about where you want to fly and to ask for suggestions on one of the many Space-A Facebook groups. Generally, you will receive several comments, and you may even find that someone recently completed a similar trip. Some Space-A internet resources will also list Space-A trip reports written by people that used Space-A to travel around the world. You can read about their experience; how they made it work and, if you search carefully, you might find a recent report that went to the location you are considering.

You may find that you live far away from an airport that has the flights you want to take. There are some options to consider. One option is to take a Space-A flight from close to your location to the Space-A airport that has the flights you want to take. Another option is to fly commercial or to take some other form of transportation to get to your desired Space-A airport. For instance, during one Space-A adventure, we left our vehicle at Dover AFB and flew to Ramstein, Germany. After touring Europe, we ended up in Rota, Spain, and caught a Space-A flight to San Diego, California. We reserved a one-way rental car from San Diego to Travis Air Force Base outside Fairfield, California, which is northeast of San Francisco. From there we eventually caught a Space-A flight back to Dover to pick up our vehicle.

You simply must have a certain level of flexibility when attempting to fly Space-A. Even after carefully planning your route, you may find out that Space-A is not cooperating with your plans. An example of this is when we drove the family from Washington D.C. to Dover AFB with the plan to fly to Germany and have a fun vacation. We knew there were several flights going to Germany in the next few days. But unfortunately, most of these flights were either canceled or didn't have enough seats for the four of us. As I was burning up my vacation days (military leave), we followed our back-up plan and drove to Canada instead.

After determining which airport you plan to fly out of using Space-A, you also need to ensure that you can get back. Just like you researched the departure airport, you should also make the same effort to research the airport you plan to use to get back home. You may find out after arriving at your destination that there are no return flights available during the time you want to come home. For instance, when we landed in San Diego, we found out there was no open passenger terminal where we could ask about Space-A flights. That airport had very limited Space-A operations. After some research, we determined that leaving San Diego using Space-A would not happen in the next few days and we had to make other plans. There were several times during our overseas Space-A adventures that our only intent was to get back anywhere stateside so that at least we could avoid paying for international commercial airline tickets.

When planning your route, you also need to consider any holidays or heavy travel times. Some Space-A terminals will reduce the number of flights during certain holidays. There are also certain travel seasons where Space-A is heavily utilized like the beginning and end of summer for travel to Europe. Doing your research by contacting terminals, reading Space-A websites and using social media can help you determine whether you are going to be in heavy competition for limited Space-A seats. This is especially true if you are retired military in Category VI and competing with all the other Space-A travelers in higher categories.

Check Travel Documents

The one area that can complicate Space-A travel is not having the proper documentation. The most important document is your DoD identification (ID) card. Active duty military or DoD civilians will have Common Access Cards (CAC), retired military will have a blue or red DD Form 2 card, reserves (those who do not have a CAC) will have a green DD Form 2 card, and dependents will have tan DD Form 1173 card. Not having the proper documentation can prevent you from using Space-A.

You will want to have your AMC Form 140, Space Available Travel Request that shows that you requested Space-A travel. Most importantly, the request should have a marking that indicates the date and time that you submitted the form. This information will determine your priority within your travel category. The earlier you submitted your request, the higher your priority for getting a Space-A seat. If you submitted your AMC Form 140 online or even through an email, make sure you have a copy of the paperwork along with the date and time of when you submitted the request. We would always print out our travel request which was in the form of an email and it would contain the date and time of when the email was sent. Then, when we got to the passenger terminal, the staff would generally update our date and time if it was not correct in the system based on what we provided.

If you are traveling overseas you want to have a passport and a possible visa. The State Department handles U.S. passports which are valid for 10 years for those 16 years old and older. Some countries require that your passport is valid at least six months beyond the dates of your trip. The State Department also has an international travel website that contains helpful travel information such as a traveler's checklist to find out about factors to consider before you go on your trip as well as safety and security information. The Country Information section of the website allows you to explore information regarding each country you plan to visit. The pages include travel advisory levels (1-4), vaccination requirements, fact sheets and also any tourist visa requirements. For example, Australia has a visa requirement and has an Electronic Travel Authority which allows certain individuals to electronically apply for the visa with a $20 AUD fee. As an additional safety measure, you may want to consider the Smart Traveler Enrollment Program (STEP) when traveling overseas. It is a free service that allows U.S. citizens traveling or living abroad to receive the latest security updates from the nearest U.S. embassy or consulate.

If you are considering driving while overseas, you may want to obtain an international driving permit (IDP). An IDP is a valid form of identification in 150 countries worldwide and contains your name, photo and driver information. It translates your identification information into 10 languages. The American Automobile Association and the American Automobile Touring Alliance can issue IDP's. We never obtained an IDP during our past travels but plan to for our next extended trip.

Some people will bring their vaccination record with them during their overseas travel. This may be helpful if traveling to a country that has a certain vaccination requirement. For instance, several countries require proof of a Yellow Fever vaccination from U.S. travelers. Regardless, it is prudent to have current vaccinations before traveling. We were never asked for proof of vaccinations during our travels given our particular destinations.

Remember that it is your responsibility to verify you have the correct documentation and it is current for the entire duration of your trip. Not having the correct paperwork could result in not being allowed entry at your travel destination or a seat on a flight.

Register

You have several choices when registering for Space-A travel. Your choices include using an automated Space-A email sign-up form, completing an official AMC Form 140, Space Available Travel Request, or just sending an email with all the pertinent information.

The AMC Space-A travel page contains a link for their automated Space-A Email Sign-up Form. When you click on the link it will take you to the AMC Space-A travel request sign-up form page. You will need to provide the following information:

- Name
- Rank/Grade
- Branch of Service
- Travel Status Category (1-6)
- Number of Seats Required
- List Names of any Dependents Traveling and Dependent Passport Type
- Email Address
- Leave Start and End Dates for Active Duty Only
- Departure Location
- Country Destination Choices (Select USA for CONUS Locations)
- Border Clearance Requirements

Once you complete the requested information and click send, your information is emailed to the departure passenger terminal location that you chose on the form. This service is provided as a convenience but AMC is not directly involved in the registration process. The departure passenger terminal should receive your request and provide you with a confirmation email. If you do not receive an email confirmation, you should contact the passenger terminal to ensure that they received your sign-up request. Be sure to write down the date/time and person you spoke with as additional confirmation. AMC suggests that you print out your email confirmation and bring it with you to the passenger terminal. The AMC passenger service agent will use the date and time shown on your email header to establish your date and time of sign-up.

When you actually arrive at the passenger terminal you will want to confirm that you are registered with the correct sign-up date and time. You will be able to change your country's destination choices at the terminal if needed. There is a section in the registration process that asks about border clearance requirements. Fortunately, we never had any issues with border clearance requirements but detailed information on this topic will be discussed in the Registration chapter.

When completing the sign-up form, do not provide any personally identifiable information (PII) such as social security numbers. Ensure that you register for Space-A flights at all potential terminals that you may visit, both arrival and departure. For instance, if I planned to travel to Germany, I would register with a few potential departure terminals in the United States and then I would also select several terminals in Europe including Germany, Spain and Italy. You increase your flexibility by registering at multiple passenger terminals; you may discover that some terminals do not have any flights whereas a nearby terminal has the flight you want. If you did not register early, there may be several other passengers higher on the list in your same category. Depending on your category, you may be able to register for Space-A flights as soon as 60 days before your expected date of travel. For instance, most retirees will sign up about 50-55 days before their planned travel date, as those who are on the list for longer will board before others in the same category. However, active duty military cannot sign up for Space-A until the start of their leave date.

An alternative to the AMC automated Space-A Email Sign-up Form is to use the Space-A Sign-up Request Form that is provided by Rob G. at Take-a-Hop. This is the primary way that we have registered for all of our Space-A travel. The website uses the same concept as the AMC form. You enter all the requested information and then the form is sent by email to all of the passenger terminals you selected. Since I would receive a copy of the sent email in my email folder, I would print that email out as proof of my registration with the email header date and time stamp. Sometimes my sign-up information was not correct when I went to see the AMC passenger service agent but they would always correct the information once I provided them with the email documentation.

Another way you can register for Space-A travel is to complete the AMC Form 140, Space Available Travel Request, and either email it or drop it off in person at your desired AMC passenger terminal. The final way to register is to simply send an email to the desired AMC passenger terminal and include all the necessary information in the body of the email. You will need to provide all the information that is listed above. The AMC Space-A travel page includes a link that contains current passenger terminal contact information with the email sign-up address for all passenger terminals. For more details concerning registration, see the Registration chapter.

Check-In

On the day of your scheduled flight, call the passenger terminal to confirm that the flight is still scheduled, has available seats for Space-A passengers and find out the Space-A showtime. You can also check the passenger terminal Facebook site to ensure that the flight information is still valid but it may not be as current as what an AMC passenger service agent can provide. Space-A seats are normally identified as early as 3-4 hours and as late as 30 minutes prior to departure. It is worth your time to arrive early. I have seen scheduled flight departure times suddenly shift two hours earlier than originally scheduled. All those travelers who arrived later or left the terminal for a short time were simply out of luck.

Once you arrive at the passenger terminal, go to the counter to mark yourself present and review the latest updated flight information. Make sure that the passenger terminal has the correct date of your sign-up as an incorrect date could result in someone else getting your seat. Once roll call starts, the order of passengers on the list will not be changed. Ensure you do not exceed baggage weight limits for your given flight and are not traveling with any prohibited items. AMC adheres to TSA guidance concerning prohibited items. AMC is also required to follow TSA procedures regarding passenger screening. Recheck that you have all the necessary documents. Await your Space-A call and follow instructions given to you by the passenger service agents. You should be ready for immediate processing and boarding if your name is called. If you are placing your vehicle in long term parking ensure that you registered your vehicle with the front counter and have the car secured at least one hour before the scheduled roll call. Most passenger terminals will have overhead monitors with the latest flight information. Check the schedule frequently as flight schedules and roll call can change without notice. You need to ensure that you can hear your name if it is announced. If your name is announced but you do not hear it, the agents will simply move on to the next passengers on the list. This can easily happen if you have a difficult to pronounce last name or are at a terminal that is crowded and loud (mostly commercial airports). This happened to us once attempting to get on a Space-A flight at BWI airport. We did not get on the flight. Most terminals will have a printout of all registered passengers listed by category and so you can determine what position you are on the list.

Fly

If you are not called for your desired flight, you will need to decide whether to return home or attempt to get on another fight at your current passenger terminal or possibly another terminal nearby. If you decide to attempt to get on another Space-A flight, you will need to let the counter agent know your plans. Your registration date and time will still remain the same as well as your original category. If you are selected for a flight you will check any baggage. If you are flying in a military aircraft you may be given the opportunity to pay for boxed lunches; this is optional. The quality of the boxed lunches will vary depending on the passenger terminal but generally includes a sandwich, drink, candy and fruit. If you are flying a commercial charter aircraft, also known as Patriot Express, you will be asked to pay a small fee around $25-$35 (head taxes $18.60, stateside segment fee $4.20, federal inspection fees). Once you arrive at your destination, ensure that you are properly registered so you can return home.

Registration

The basics of Space-A registration were covered in the Space-A Process chapter. Remember that the chapter mentioned three options for registration: 1) use an automated Space-A email sign-up form, 2) complete an official AMC Form 140, or 3) just send an email to the terminal with all the necessary information. This chapter provides additional details regarding the registration process.

Remote Sign-up

Remote sign-up is a means of registering for Space-A travel without actually being physically present in the passenger terminal. Remote sign-up allows passengers to sign-up for Space-A travel by emailing or faxing copies of necessary information to the departure passenger terminal. The email or fax data header will establish the date and time of sign-up. Active duty personnel cannot submit their paperwork any earlier than the effective date of leave. Although rare, mailed in entries will also be accepted and the date and time for sign-up will be the time it is received at the passenger service counter.

Self Sign-up

Self sign-up is a program that allows passengers to sign-up at a passenger terminal without waiting in line. Most locations provide self sign-up counters with easy to follow instructions for registration. Active duty personnel must ensure sign-up takes place no earlier than the effective date of leave. If your travel will take you to a foreign country, ensure border clearance documentation is up to date. If you are unsure of specific requirements, you can speak with a passenger service agent.

Space-A Register

Each passenger terminal maintains a Space-A register organized by priority category and the date and time of registration for travel. The register is located in the terminal and updated daily. If you cannot locate the register, ask a passenger service agent. Travelers may call the passenger terminal to ensure they are listed in the register and ask where they are listed compared to all others.

When to Sign-up

When you can sign up for Space-A is based on your eligibility status. Travelers in active duty status can only register for Space-A when their leave or pass begins. This does not necessarily mean when your leave or pass is approved as the start date may be later. You also need to remain in leave or pass status for your entire time period that you are utilizing Space-A. That is why it is so critical for active duty travelers to ensure they have sufficient time on their pass or leave to catch a return trip.

Retirees can sign-up for Space-A travel at any time. All unaccompanied dependents require a signed and dated Space-A letter for a valid sign-up. Dependents of deployed members using the Category III or Category IV deployed sponsor program cannot sign-up any earlier than 10 days before the member deploys (even if they have a memo issued earlier than the 10 days) and cannot travel before the first day of the sponsor's deployment.

The earlier you sign-up the more seniority you will have within your travel category. Your goal should be to have as much seniority (days) on the Space-A register without having your sign-up expire when you are competing for a flight. All passengers should sign-up at every location where they might need to compete for seats which means Active Duty should sign-up at potential departure and return locations as soon as their leave status begins. Registrations are only valid for 60 days. The exception for active duty is that their Space-A travel period is the same as the duration of their leave.

Many retirees and unaccompanied dependents plan their sign-up date so that they have approximately 50-55 days on a location's Space-A register on the first day that they plan to attempt travel. That allows them to have subsequent opportunities before their sign-up expires. Once their registration expires, they will need to reregister and will go to the bottom of their respective category.

How to Sign-up

You need to register (sign-up) for Space-A travel at each location where you plan to compete for seats. You can sign-up at multiple locations at any time. Each location maintains its own sign-up register so you must sign-up at each location for which you plan to travel. Your sign-ups at different locations are not affected by what you do at a particular location.

Experienced Space-A travelers will usually call to verify their sign-up was successfully received and entered into the system. It is a good idea to print out copies of your email sign-up receipts and bring them along in case you arrive at a departure point and you are not registered. Passenger service agents will normally honor your hand-carried registration showing your original day and time of sign-up. Once you are added to the Space-A register, you are eligible for any flights that depart that location only for the duration of your sign-up. You need to sign-up at other locations if necessary.

A DoD ID number is required by all passengers for Space-A travel, except retirees with an ID card only showing a social security number (SSN). It is HQ AMC policy that DoD ID Number or SSN disclosure is not required for remote sign-up yet some AMC detachments do not comply with the policy. Some locations may ignore your sign-up without a DoD ID number or SSN. In those cases, you can either use your passport number or a dummy SSN as a placeholder for your

SSN and then update your registration once you are at the passenger terminal. For instance, you can create a SSN but include your last four digits of your correct SSN (XXX-XX-1234). I normally just include my last four digits of my SSN and passport number when registering remotely and never had an issue. But now with a DoD ID number available, I prefer to use that rather than my SSN. Fortunately, my retiree ID card contains my DoD ID number.

Note that some passenger terminals will not accept remote sign-up and require travelers to sign-up in person. This generally occurs on most Navy bases but there are some exceptions such as Norfolk, Jacksonville, Naples, Sigonella and Rota which act as AMC terminals. For instance, we were able to remotely sign-up in both Sigonella and Rota.

Sign-up Form - Country Choices

Country choices or codes are countries, not specific installations or locations. But some OCONUS U.S. states and territories are included such as Hawaii, Alaska, and Guam. Select the top five countries or OCONUS destinations you want to visit. For all the old-timers, AMC stopped using "ALL" as a valid Country Choice. Your country choices can be changed when you arrive at an AMC departure location and passengers will not be penalized when changing their destination. For CONUS locations select "USA." You can write the name of the country but if you prefer to use the code, *Air Mobility Command Instruction 24-101 Volume 14, Table A7.1*, contains all the country codes for Space-A sign-up. These instructions also contain a wealth of other information concerning passenger travel.

Multiple Location Sign-up

You can sign-up at any or all locations where you think you will travel including for your return trip. Your sign-up is unique to that location.

Once registered, you will generally remain on the Space-A register for that particular location for 60 days, the duration of your leave orders or authorization, or until you get manifested on a flight at that location, whichever occurs first. When you depart a location, you will be removed from that location's list. Your sign-ups at the other locations are not affected by what you do at another location.

Signing-up More Than Once at the Same Location

You can only have one current sign-up at a specific location. The second submission will normally overwrite the first submission and your sign-up date and time will reset. If you have to sign-up twice at the same location then annotate your change of plans in the remarks of your sign-up request or in your email. It is always prudent to confirm that the latest registration was correctly received and recorded by speaking with a passenger service agent.

Changing Your Seat Requirement

If you are unsure how many people in your group will be traveling Space-A, list all potential travelers in the Space-A request. When you actually arrive at the passenger terminal you will be able to adjust the number of requested travelers.

Children and Infant Seat Requirements

Every passenger, to include children and infants, are required to have an assigned seat; be sure to include all members of your group in your sign-up request. For example, if there is one Space-A seat remaining and you and your infant are next on the list, you will be skipped and the next single passenger will be selected.

Duration of Sign-up

The length of time that your registration is valid will depend on your status and the particular passenger terminal. Active duty sign-ups are normally valid for either 45 or 60 days or the duration of the service member's leave, whichever date occurs first. This also applies to reservists on active duty for 30 days or more. Active duty military members whose leave orders have expired shall be allowed to remain on the Space-A register if they are attempting to have their leave extended. These personnel will not be allowed to utilize Space-A travel until their leave is extended unless there are extenuating circumstances and they obtain approval by the appropriate official.

All other sign-ups (retired and unaccompanied dependents) are normally valid for 45 or 60 days. Authorized Reserve Component members in their normal reserve status will also have 45 or 60 days; this also applies to reservists on active duty for 30 days or less. Most Air Force and AMC run passenger terminals will have a 60-day valid registration. Navy facilities will typically validate registrations for only 45 days. For example, Naval Air Station North Island Air Terminal states that registrations are only valid for 45 days. Per the website Spacea.net, Naval Air Station Oceana in Virginia does not have remote sign-up, requires 72-hour notice for Space-A sign-up, and is handled either in person or by calling the terminal with your request. There will always be some exceptions to the general 45 to 60-day validity period.

Your sign-up expires at each location 60 days (or 45 days or leave expiration as applicable) after you signed up at that particular location. Once expired, you need to submit another sign-up for that location and start over. Once you are manifested (assigned a seat) on a flight and depart from a location you will be removed from the Space-A register at that location. For example, if you are a retiree and sign-up for Space-A travel with Dover Air Force Base and Ramstein Air Force Base on January 1st, your registration will be valid for 60 days (January

1 till March 1) at both locations. If you happened to depart Dover on February 15th, then you left on the 46th day of your registration (Jan 1-31 + Feb 1-15 = 46 total days). Once you leave Dover, your registration with Dover is no longer valid. Your Ramstein registration is also 46 days old which means you will have 14 days left on your Ramstein registration (max 60 day – 46 used days = 14 days remaining).

Space-A Registration Email Verification

Space-A passenger terminals receive many remote requests for Space-A travel. A significant amount of the requests will never be used. Thus, some locations do not enter the information into their database or acknowledge the sign-up with an email reply. You can call each passenger terminal to confirm receipt but that can be cumbersome if you sent out your requests to several terminals across various time zones. Another method to confirm your registration/sign-up, is to make a copy of your email request and bring it with you to the passenger terminal as proof of the date and time you submitted your request. You can simply go to the sent folder of your email program which will contain the date/time stamp of submission or carbon copy (CC) yourself in the original email request. Most locations will honor your email printouts. We have never had an issue using this method. You may also want to check your junk or spam folder for any confirmation emails.

Customs and Immigration Border Clearance

When you attempt to register or sign-up for Space-A travel, one of the questions asked is, "Are your border clearance documents current?" You can disregard this question if you are traveling CONUS. However, it is important for OCONUS travel. The sign-up form gives the general disclaimer: "Border clearance requirements vary by country. If you are unsure of the specific requirements for your desired destination, contact the nearest AMC passenger terminal for assistance."

The basic idea behind this issue is that every country will have certain requirements to be able to enter their country. Some of the conditions of entry may be as follows:

- Proof of United States citizenship
- Passport
- Visa
- Yellow fever vaccination required if entering from an infected area
- Cholera immunization required if entering from an infected area
- Bilingual leave authorization in Portuguese and English or French and English may be used in lieu of a passport for military personnel
- Tourist card recommended instead of visa
- Preclearance from United States Defense Attaché Office (USDAO)
- Leave authorization containing the following statement may be used in lieu of a passport for military personnel: "La persona a quien esta orden pertenezca esta autorizada por las autoridades militares competentes de los Estados Unidos de America para entrar o salir de Espana en mision oficial vestido

de civil o militar"

Some additional country-specific requirements are:

- Passport or visa requirement does not apply for DoD personnel stationed in Germany
- When traveling to Japan for tourist purposes, a visa is not required for U.S. passport holders with a valid passport if the length of stay is 90 days or less
- Tourist visas are available upon arrival in Panama
- When traveling to Incirlik AB, Turkey, for tourist purposes, the possibility exists that you may be unable to obtain a gate pass as such documents are issued by the Turkish Air Force and are required to exit or enter the installation

Defense Transportation Regulation, Part V, Department of Defense Customs and Border Clearance Policies and Procedures provides some general guidance but the *DoD Electronic Foreign Clearance Guide (FCG)* is only available from a U.S. government computer. The State Department has an international travel website with a Country Information section that provides country-specific entry and exit requirements that you can research before starting your trip. We never had any issues with border clearance but we generally flew into countries without a visa requirement and always had a passport. If you have any concerns, ask the passenger terminal agent.

Passports and Visa Requirements

When traveling outside the United States, it is wise to have a passport. You can obtain passport information from the U.S. Department of State, Bureau of Consular Affairs and start the process online at travel.state.gov. The cost of a U.S. passport depends on the type of passport you request and how quickly you need it. If the passport is issued to someone under the age of 16, then the passport is valid for five years; otherwise, it will be valid for 10 years. Some countries require that your passport is valid for at least six months beyond the dates of your trip so be careful if traveling and your passport is about to expire. You can get a passport with either a 28-page or 52-page book. If you plan to do a lot of traveling in foreign countries where they will stamp your visa pages, get the larger book because once your visa pages are fully stamped, you will be required to get a new passport.

An alternative to a regular passport is a passport card, but it very limiting. The passport card is the wallet-size travel document that can only be used to re-enter the United States at land border-crossings and sea ports-of-entry from Canada, Mexico, the Caribbean, and Bermuda. The card provides a less expensive, smaller, and convenient alternative to the passport book for those who travel frequently to these destinations by land or by sea. The passport card cannot be used for international travel by air.

If you need to change your name on your passport because of circumstances such as being recently married or divorced, there are two procedures depending on the issued date of your passport. If you are changing your name within one year of the date your passport was issued, you will need to complete Form DS-5504: Application for a U.S. Passport: Name Change, Data Correction, and Limited Passport Book Replacement. You will not be charged a fee for this service. If you are changing your name more than a year after your passport was issued, you must submit Form DS-82: Application for Passport by Mail. You must pay all applicable fees to renew your passport.

Travelers on active duty should consult the Foreign Clearance Guide for Passport and other requirements if traveling in a leave status to foreign countries.

No-Fee Passport

In order to obtain a no-fee passport, you have to fall into one of the eligible categories.

- A U.S. government employee or service member on official business
- A dependent of that employee or service member traveling with the employee on government business
- A relative of a deceased member of the U.S. Armed Forces going overseas to visit grave sites or memorials

If you qualify for a no-fee passport, it does not replace your regular, paid passport. The no-fee passport works only for official business connected to the granting of the fee waiver. Most no-fee passports are only issued to those going overseas for the express purpose of working in some capacity for the U.S. Government. Those holding a battle monument no-fee passport cannot use it for anything other than visiting overseas memorial sites.

These no-fee passports are issued by the Special Issuance Agency of the U.S. State Department, and are assigned according to three types that are determined by the nature of the applicant's work; regular no-fee, diplomatic, and official. The type of no-fee passport depends upon the reason for the government worker's travel and is determined by the Special Issuance Agency. If you happen to be among those who qualify for a no-fee passport and are authorized to travel with dependents, your dependents will be issued no-fee passports as well; they will not be included under yours.

You should know when and how you can use your no-fee passport overseas. Your no-fee passport is for use during the commission of official duties only, and it is generally prohibited for use in any kind of personal travel. If you plan on doing personal travel while on an official overseas assignment, you should use your regular fee passport. You can carry both passports with you, so you should never have a problem as long as you use them appropriately.

The form to obtain a no-fee passport is DD Form 1056, Authorization for Apply for a "No-Fee" Passport and/or Request for Visa, and is covered in *DoD 1000.21, DoD Passport and Passport Agent Services*. This directive establishes DoD policy that U.S. no-fee passports are official documents of the U.S. Government and remain at all times the property of the United States. Passports shall be surrendered to the Government on-demand by an authorized representative of the U.S. Government.

The Foreign Clearance Guide (FCG) is the document Passenger Service Agents normally use to determine if your border clearance documents are valid. The FCG states that "service members and their eligible family members stationed abroad and issued no-fee passports may use these passports for incidental personal travel during the period of their overseas assignment. While outside the United States, no-fee passports may be used for incidental personal travel between foreign destinations providing the foreign government concerned accepts no-fee passports for personal travel. If the foreign government does not accept no-fee passports for personal travel, travelers must obtain regular fee passports at their own expense." The FCG defines "Incidental Travel" as "Travel DoD-sponsored travelers for purposes other than in the discharge of U.S. Government business." So if you are assigned overseas with a no-fee passport and plan to conduct some Space-A travel to other foreign countries, you can attempt to use your no-fee passport on your travels but there is no guarantee that they will be accepted and it may be prudent to just obtain a regular passport for your travels.

Visas

A visa is an endorsement on a passport indicating that the holder is allowed to enter, leave, or stay for a specified period of time in a country. U.S. citizens may need a visa issued by the embassy of the country they wish to visit. Some countries allow visas to be obtained online or through third-party contractors rather than through a consulate or embassy. In order to determine whether a particular country has a visa requirement for U.S. citizens, review the country information available on the U.S. Department of State Bureau of Consular Affairs website. In addition to possible visa requirements, you will also learn about safety and security information to help you assess the possible risks of travel. Some information found on the country-specific international travel pages include:

- Tourist visa requirement
- Blank passport page requirement
- Vaccination requirement
- Currency restrictions
- Entry and exit requirements
- Local laws
- Travel and transportation
- Fact sheets
- Travel advisory levels

1 – Exercise normal precautions
2 – Exercise increased caution
3 – Reconsider travel
4 – Do not travel

For example, if you navigate to the U.S. Department of State Bureau of Consular Affairs website and select "Vietnam," you will find a variety of helpful information on the country of Vietnam. For instance, the country of Vietnam has a tourist visa requirement. The entry requirement is a valid passport and a visa (or pre-approval for a visa on arrival). The passport must be valid for six months beyond your planned stay and must have at least one blank visa page. The Consular Affairs website will also provide the Embassy of Vietnam website link to ensure travelers can obtain the most current information. There is also a message stating that the Government of Vietnam has authorized some businesses and travel agencies to arrange for pre-approval for a "visa on arrival" at the airport but because some U.S. citizens have reported being charged unexpectedly high fees and additional charges upon landing in Vietnam, it is recommended that travelers obtain a visa directly from an embassy or consulate of Vietnam prior to arrival. Vietnam also allows U.S. citizens to apply online for a single E-visa on the Vietnam Immigration website.

Another example is for entry to Australia. You must have a valid U.S. passport and a visa or approved Electronic Travel Authority (ETA) to enter Australia. Most U.S. passport holders traveling to Australia for tourism or business purposes for less than 90 days can obtain an ETA. The ETA is an electronic label-free visa and can be obtained at the ETA website for a small service fee. As you can see, every country will have its own requirements and it is prudent to check the country page at the Consular Affairs website for every country you plan to visit.

European Travel Information and Authorization System (ETIAS)

The European Travel Information and Authorization System (ETIAS) visa waiver will be a travel requirement to visit Europe starting in 2024. U.S. citizens who wish to travel to and around Europe will have to apply online for an ETIAS visa waiver. ETIAS is an integrated visa waiver system implemented to increase security and provide more efficient management of Europe's borders, similar to the U.S. Electronic System for Travel Authorization (ESTA). An ETIAS authorization will be required for every American citizen traveling to Europe for short-term stays of up to 90 days.

The ETIAS authorization is not a visa. There is no need to go to a consulate to make an application, no biometric data is collected and significantly less information is gathered than during a visa application procedure.

American citizens will be able to obtain the ETIAS travel authorization by completing the online form with their personal information and by answering security questions. The ETIAS travel authorization will be a multiple entry authorization valid for 3 years. If your application is approved you will receive a confirmation email with the ETIAS for Europe. If your application is denied you will receive an email with a written explanation for the refusal. While children under the age of 18 will be required to have an ETIAS, they will not be charged the application fee.

Because the ETIAS is valid for short-term stays of up to 90 days for both leisure and business travelers, you will be able to re-enter Europe multiple times within that three-year period without renewing it, as long as your stay doesn't exceed 90 days within a 180-day period. Those who want to study or work in Europe will need to apply for a proper visa.

Americans will also need to provide the Member State of intended first entry, and they must enter the Schengen Area through that country. Providing the Member State of intended first entry simply means which country you first plan on entering on your arrival to Europe. The ETIAS visa waiver will be valid to enter countries that are part of the Schengen Area but not the European Union (EU), which means, that U.S. citizens will be able to travel to these countries without the need for any additional travel documents or permissions.

Both Schengen countries and EU countries are European countries. However, not all EU nations are part of the Schengen Zone. The European Union is a unique economic and political union of 28 member states that have developed a single market. Currently, 19 EU member states use the Euro (EUR – €) as their currency.

The Schengen Area is comprised of 26 European countries of which only 4 are not members of the EU. These four countries are Iceland, Norway, Switzerland, and Liechtenstein. Schengen area countries have abolished passports, and any other type of border control at their shared borders also referred to as internal borders. While Romania, Bulgaria, Croatia, and Cyprus are not currently Schengen countries, they are in the process of joining and will be subject to the same requirements once they do.

There are still many European nations that are not part of the Schengen Zone which means you can still travel to Albania, Andorra, Armenia, Azerbaijan, Belarus, Bosnia and Herzegovina, Georgia, Kosovo, Macedonia, Moldova, Montenegro, Serbia, Turkey, and Ukraine without an ETIAS. Having an ETIAS does not preclude passport requirements.

ETIAS Countries include the following:

- Austria
- Belgium
- Czech Republic
- Denmark
- Estonia
- Finland
- France
- Germany
- Greece

- Hungary
- Italy
- Latvia
- Lithuania
- Luxembourg
- Malta
- Netherlands
- Poland
- Portugal
- Slovakia
- Slovenia
- Spain
- Sweden
- Iceland
- Liechtenstein
- Norway
- Switzerland
- San Marino
- Vatican City
- Monaco

Space-A Facebook Groups

Facebook groups are an excellent way to share information and ask questions related to Space-A travel. Even if you are not an active Facebook user, it is worth establishing an account to gain access to the knowledge that members of these groups share. Most of these groups are "closed" which means you have to request to join the group. Generally joining the group is fairly easy; you just answer a few questions and agree to comply with their standards of conduct.

I am constantly surprised how many travelers are brand new to the Space-A experience and are attempting their first Space-A journey. These groups are really helpful if you have a specific trip in mind and plan to visit a particular country or destination. Simply posting your intentions on the group and asking for advice will solicit several helpful comments. Particularly valuable is when someone responds who has just traveled Space-A to the same destination and can provide current, helpful information such as flight details, passenger terminal procedures, best local hotels, restaurants, and venues. For instance, I was considering visiting Singapore and when I went on the Facebook Space-A groups I found out about regular flights between Singapore and Japan and what was required to gain access to the passenger terminal in Singapore. I also collected information about local hotels, transportation and activities. What was even more interesting was that there is a Facebook Space-A group just for Singapore, the Paya Lebar Air Base Singapore Space A Forum. There are general Space-A Facebook groups but also very specific Space-A Facebook groups for a particular passenger terminal or country. Some of the Space-A Facebook groups are as follows:

Space-A DoD Travelers of USA

This is a private group with more than 79,000 members. It is the largest Space-A group on Facebook. Members use it to ask questions and receive crowd-sourced answers from other members. Several Space-A experts moderate the group and often post updates on significant changes to Space-A policies. The group has 17 administrators and eight moderators.

www.facebook.com/groups/ 325711150854371/?ref=group_browse

Spacea.net

This Facebook page is a non-official volunteer page designed to help fellow military (active duty, dependents and retirees) and other uniformed service members understand how to use military Space-A travel. Their disclaimer is to verify everything with current regulations and policy before you travel. It is a public Facebook page founded in 2005. The only listed team member is John Doyle.

www.facebook.com/spacea.net

Military Space Available Travel

This is a private group that is designed to bring together those that are eligible and interested in Space-A travel on military aircraft. The administrators include Dirk Pepperd, Kathy Heidt Pepperd, Marea Nelson Bass and Carole Green. The group has over 13,000 members.

www.facebook.com/groups/43633027637/?ref=group_browse

CAT VI Retirees Space-A

This is a private group with over 9,000 members. It was created in 2014 by Roy Deal. This group is an offshoot of Space-A DoD Travelers of USA, but it is specifically for retirees. It is much smaller than the main group, but the information is focused on retirees. The group has nine administrators and nine moderators.

www.facebook.com/groups/ 16728793162273906/?ref=linked_groups_hscroll

Trip Reports Archives

This is a private group with over 1,000 members. This group focuses on Space-A trip reports and is great resource to gather ideas about possible future Space-A trips and also to learn from others who recently completed a documented Space-A adventure. The group has six administrators and two moderators.

www.facebook.com/groups/ 488886477796513/?ref=group_browse

Space-A Adventure U.S. Trip Reports

This is a private group with over 4,000 members. This group focuses on Space-A trip reports and has ten administrators and one moderator.

www.facebook.com/groups/1176693559010551

Paya Lebar Air Base Singapore Space A Forum

This is a private group that focuses on Paya Lebar Air Base, a military airbase of the Republic of Singapore Air Force located at Paya Lebar, in the central-eastern part of Singapore as well as Singapore Changi International Airport, which is a major civilian airport that serves Singapore and is one of the largest transportation hubs in Asia. Paya Lebar Air Base has a regular flight rotating to Yokota Air Base which is a United States Air Force and Japan Air Self-Defense Force base in the city of Fussa in Western Tokyo, Japan. The group has nine administrators and one moderator.

www.facebook.com/groups/PayaLebar.SpaceAForum/about

U.S. Military Travelers in Japan

This group, managed by the Poppin' Smoke website, is for travelers who are interested in traveling to Japan. The group exchanges information about Space-A travel, using U.S. military facilities in Japan, and general tourism. The group has two administrators, two moderators and over 700 members.

www.facebook.com/groups/MilitaryTravelersJapan

SpaceATheWorld

This group was created and managed by an active-duty spouse who has traveled around the world using Space-A. She shares details of her trip planning and travel adventures, while encouraging group members to do the same. The group has two administrators, nine moderators, and over 13,000 members.

www.facebook.com/groups/248765535507913

There are several other available Space-A related Facebook groups. You will notice that some of the same people are administrators or moderators in the different Space-A groups. There are Space-A groups that are specific to nearly every region and passenger terminal in the world. A recommendation is to join the primary Space-A Facebook group, Space-A DoD Travelers of USA, and then you will learn about the other groups.

Space-A Websites

This chapter will discuss websites that contain general information related to Space-A travel. These websites can be a great source of Space-A information and resources. Websites that contain reference material regarding specific travel topics will be available in the references chapter.

Poppin' Smoke

Poppin' Smoke is a website for retired and soon-to-be-retired members of the military community who want to take advantage of their retirement benefits to travel. The website name comes from the military term to "pop smoke" which means to get moving or take off. The site contains a variety of travel information including Space-A travel information, blogs, and resources. The website is very modern, professionally organized, and current. It is one of the latest websites to enter the Space-A community and is garnering a lot of traffic and attention. The site is run by Stephanie Montague who is a communications consultant and freelance writer. She has written several articles pertaining to military and travel related topics in the publication MilitaryByOwner, PCSgrades, and G.I.Jobs.

www.poppinsmoke.com

SpaceA.net

SpaceA.net is an unofficial Space-A information website for members of the uniformed services. The information contained on the website is compiled from online forums, individual contributions, websites, personal knowledge, and regulations since 2001. There is a disclaimer to verify everything with current regulations and policies before you plan your travel.

The site was created when John Doyle decided to host the Space-A FAQ information previously hosted on the spacea.info website on his own website. The site has grown tremendously since its inception as a FAQ repository and now includes a large amount of detailed Space-A information.

The website includes passenger terminal locations and Space-A links, lodging, schedules, and social media pages. There is also a robust regulations, forms and letters section. The Space-A FAQs are extensive. They also manage the public Spacea.net Facebook page.

www.spacea.net

Take-a-Hop

This website is a free and private website created for friends and family who are affiliated with the U.S. Department of Defense and utilize Space-A travel. This site allows you to sign-up for Space-A travel using your computer or mobile device. The site is run by Rob G., an Air Force veteran. Rob G. created his site around 2005 when Roy Buckman's sign-up service was no longer being maintained by Military Living. He is constantly upgrading his features such as adding a fax capability for passenger terminals that did not accept emails, allowing five departure locations at one time, or creating a mobile app in 2012. Ensure you keep a copy of the sign-up email for possible verification at the passenger terminal. We used this sign-up method on several occasions without any issues. It was the quickest way to sign-up for Space-A travel before the AMC website created their own online sign-up form.

www.takeahop.com

Dirk Pepperd's Space-A Message Board

This website has been in existence for over 20 years and contains an abundant amount of information pertaining to Space-A travel. Access costs $29.95 per year and there is a 30-day trial membership program.

The original message board was created in the mid-1990s when Dirk Pepperd was on active duty, changed to a member-only discussion board in 2003 due to spammers and hackers, and finally transitioned to the current discussion forum in 2010. Dirk Pepperd is also an administrator of the "Military Space Available Travel" Facebook group.

www.pepperd.com

Military Living

Military Living Publications is a publisher of military travel information for all uniformed service members, active and retired and their family members. They have a Space-A Air section on their website that contains limited, general Space-A information by state, country, and passenger terminal. They have a travel guide FAQ and military lodging information.

Military Living took over the spacea.info website created by Roy Buckman in 2005. If you go to spacea.info, you will simply be redirected to the Military Living website. Roy Buckman created a Space-A related discussion board in the late 1990s in addition to the first online sign-up service. When Roy Buckman passed in 2005, his forum and sign-up service ceased to exist.

militaryliving.com

SpaceA.us

This basic Space-A blog run by Craig and Beth Hullinger contains a long list of Space-A related links that you can click for further information.

spacea10.blogspot.com/?view=classic

Air Mobility Command Space Available Travel Page

This website is the official United States Air Force website for AMC Space-A travel. The website contains a wealth of information concerning Space-A travel including the following:

- Travel Instructions
- Space-A Sign Up
- Passenger Terminal Social Media Sites
- Passenger Terminal Contact Information
- Travel Information Links
- Operational Security for Social Media and Travelers
- AMC Passenger Terminal Locations (Interactive Map)
- Frequently Asked Questions (FAQ) Page

www.amc.af.mil/Home/AMC-Travel-Site/AMC-Space-Available-Travel-Page

Military OneSource

This website is a DoD funded program designed to offer a wide range of individualized consultations, coaching and non-medical counseling for many aspects of military life. In the recreation, travel and shopping section, on the travel page, there is information about Space-A flights. Other information on the page includes military lodging, recreation resources, American Forces Travel, and other travel resources.

www.militaryonesource.mil/recreation-travel-shopping/travel/[1] travel-resources[2]

---

1. http://www.militaryonesource.mil/recreation-travel-shopping/travel/

2. http://www.militaryonesource.mil/recreation-travel-shopping/travel/

Basic Space-A Tips

Military OneSource is a Department of Defense funded program that provides a variety of services for members of the military and their family. They also provide some of the following general Space-A tips.

Plan to trade your time for the discounted ticket. The lower your category, the more likely it is that others in higher categories will take available seats on popular flights. Give yourself three-day buffers on each end of your travel plans to catch flights and remember that more Space-A flights tend to be scheduled on weekdays, Mondays through Fridays.

Avoid military reserve drill weekends and school breaks. Drill tends to fill military Space-A flights, and many families schedule vacations around school breaks. To avoid these, call the terminal's base to ask if the local Guard or reserve unit will be drilling the weekend you intend to leave. Then, check the Department of Defense Education Activity, or DoDEA, school calendar for seasonal school breaks.

Be willing to take Space-A flights that get you close, but not directly to, your final destination. For example, if you are traveling from the U.S. to a European destination consider grabbing a more open flight from a convenient local base to a country close to your destination, then take local civilian transportation.

Plan for every climate. You might be on a flight initially scheduled to go to Hawaii, but have an emergency reroute to Alaska to fulfill the military Space-A flight's primary mission. Readily prepare by having available clothing in different layers.

Be flexible. Make the delays and alternate routes an adventure, rather than an inconvenience. You may not have expected to go to Germany instead of Italy, but it is an opportunity for spontaneous sightseeing.

Do not expect a traditional civilian flight unless it is Patriot Express (Rotator), a commercial charter flight. Sometimes, the military contracts with a civilian airline for troop movement, making a Patriot Express flight available for Space-A. Other Space-A flights will be on large, and loud, military cargo planes, complete with harnesses for passengers during lift-off and landing.

Bring supplies for a comfortable flight. Consider taking a small sleeping bag, pillow, blankets, and even a yoga mat if you think you'll want to sleep during Space-A flights on large military planes. Some planes will have small pillows and blankets but there are no guarantees. While some crews provide military-issue earplugs for the noise, you may want to bring your own or some noise-canceling headphones. On especially loud planes, I would wear both earplugs and noise-canceling headphones. Winter hats and gloves might help too, as some planes get very cold. Bring hand wipes or sanitizer as the bathrooms on the planes may not have running water.

Pack as light as possible. Not only because there are weight restrictions on certain planes, but also to make it easier to travel once you get to your final destination. If there is a Space-A flight with weight restrictions and you pack light, you may be selected instead of other passengers that cannot travel on that particular fight due to their heavy luggage.

Some items to consider bringing on your travels include a portable charger, small flashlight, snacks, water bottle, a quick-dry towel, and some carabiners to help with fastening items while in the plane or to your backpack/luggage/belt loop.

General Space-A Information

Travelers who may not be familiar with the Space-A system often do not know which questions to ask to get the right information. To help make your traveling easier, the next few chapters include some common Space-A topics organized into separate categories.

Distinctions of Rank, Component, or Branch

Transportation opportunities will be provided on an equitable basis without regard to rank or grade, military or civilian, or branch of uniformed service. No distinction is made between members retired from the Reserve Component and members retired from active duty.

Flying on a CONUS Segment

Individuals traveling to or from an OCONUS location may travel on any CONUS leg segment (i.e., on a flight with en route stops) only when there is no change of aircraft or mission number. So if you are only eligible to fly from OCONUS to CONUS but not CONUS to CONUS and your flight goes from Ramstein, Germany to San Diego, California, with a refueling stop in Norfolk, Virginia, you will not be asked to terminate your flight in Norfolk unless there is a change in plans and a different plane will be going from Norfolk to San Diego or the mission number changes.

Clothing

When civilian clothing is worn, it should not conflict with accepted attire in the overseas country of departure, transit, or destination. For example, some countries do not allow the wear of camouflage patterns or clothing as civilian attire, clothing with negative political statements against the country, or clothing disparaging country leaders.

Retaining a Spot in an Aircraft Until the Final Destination

Once accepted for movement, a Space-A passenger will not be bumped by another Space-A passenger, regardless of category. But on a case-by-case basis, the local installation commander may change the priority of movement of any Space-A traveler for emergency or humanitarian reasons when the circumstances fully support such an exception.

Holding a Particular Seat in the Aircraft

Space available seats may not be reserved or blocked for use at en route stops along mission routes. This means that if your flight makes a stop before your final destination and you are asked to deplane, you cannot hold your current seats for when you come back on the plane.

Passenger Conduct

Instances of unacceptable passenger conduct or behavior that warrant consideration for removal of Space-A privileges will be processed in accordance with *Volume 14 of AMC Instruction 24-101*. Such behavior can include being visible drunk or on drugs, being extremely argumentative with the passenger terminal agents, or fighting with other personnel.

Leave or Pass Status

Uniformed services members must be in a valid leave, pass, or non-duty status to register for travel and remain in such status for the entire period of travel. If passengers subsequently present leave orders, they must re-sign up with a new effective date and time consistent with their leave forms.

DoD civilian employees, when given any of the Space-A privileges, must be in a leave or non-duty (i.e., weekend or holiday) status to register for Space-A travel. If in non-duty status, leave must be approved for the first normal working day following the non-duty period. Employees will be on leave status while awaiting travel and for the entire period of travel.

Traveling in Uniform

Each service determines its own travel uniform policies as well as *DoDD 4500.54E*. Currently, all services except the Marine Corps permit appropriate civilian attire on DoD-owned or controlled aircraft. When civilian clothing is worn it should be in good taste and not in conflict with accepted attire in the overseas country of departure, transit, or destination, as defined by the DoD Foreign Clearance Guide. It should also be capable of keeping you warm especially on military aircraft. Passengers are also reminded that high heeled, open-toed and "five finger" styled shoes may not be worn on military aircraft.

Space-A Costs

Space-A passengers will be assessed a Federal Inspection Fee if they travel on a commercial mission arriving in the United States from overseas. A Head Tax is another fee that applies to Space-A passengers who arrive or depart the Customs Territories of the United States (CTUS) to or from overseas locations on these missions. There may be expenses for phone calls to find out about flights, a room for the night along the way, or a bus fare to get from one base to another. Passengers can limit these costs depending on how frugal they are (e.g. take a bus versus renting a car) and if opportunities for savings are available (i.e. base lodging versus a commercial hotel room). Meals may be purchased at a nominal fee at most air terminals while traveling on military aircraft. Meal service on contracted commercial charter flights (Patriot Express) is complimentary.

AMC Terminal Facilities

Facilities at most of the larger military terminals are generally the same as commercial facilities. Facilities on base may include AAFES/NEX, barber shops, snack bars, television, traveler assistance, United Services Organization (USO) lounges, and Family Lounges. The type of facility available will vary according to the terminal size and location. Most AMC Passenger Terminals close overnight so Space-A travelers must be prepared for lodging expenses.

Best Time to Travel Space-A

Anytime other than peak travel and holidays (December-January and June-August) periods.

Easier Space-A Destinations

Places such as Japan, Spain, and Germany are much easier than low-frequency areas.

Travel Space-A to Alaska or South America

Travelers may obtain Space-A travel to Alaska, South America, and other interesting locations; i.e. Australia, Japan, etc. Travel to Alaska is relatively easy when departing from Travis AFB, California, and JBLM, Washington State. Travel to South America and other remote areas can be much more difficult. Infrequent flights to remote areas are primarily cargo missions and have few seats available for passenger movement. Expect long waiting periods for movement. Travelers may consider using Space-A to get as close as possible to a remote location and then using commercial transportation for the final leg of their journey.

Space-A Travel on Other than AMC flights

Travel eligibility is for all DoD-owned or controlled aircraft. AMC, however, does not always have knowledge of other commands/services' scheduled flight information.

Calling the Passenger Terminal for Flight Information

AMC can only release limited flight information for up to 72 hours. However, you are encouraged to call the passenger terminal you plan on traveling through 30-60 days before travel. The terminal will be able to discuss Space-A opportunities from their location.

Using Personal Credit Cards for Incidental AMC Travel Costs

Personal credit cards are accepted at most AMC terminals. Contact your local or departing terminal to ensure the use of a credit card service is available.

Substituting Space-A Travel for Commercial Airline Travel

Space-A travel may be a good travel choice if travelers have a flexible schedule and finances allow for a hotel stay (sometimes in a "high-cost" area) while awaiting movement. While some travelers may sign up and travel the same day, many factors could come together and make buying a commercial ticket the best or only option. Space-A travel depends on flexibility and good timing.

Determining Eligibility to Fly Space-A

The four services jointly establish Space-A eligibility. AMC's first responsibility is airlifting official DoD travelers. Space-A seats can be offered only after official duty passengers and cargo.

Duration of Remaining on the Space-A Register

All travelers using AMC passenger terminals remain on the register for 60 days after registration, for the duration of their travel authorization, or until they are selected for travel. Navy facilities will typically validate registrations for only 45 days.

Pending Base Closures and Space-A Travel

Base closures are always possible but they are generally known far in advance. This should not affect your Space-A travel as if a base is closed there will simply be no flights scheduled for that location. There were some recent closures or realignments of some bases in the past few years that altered Space-A opportunities in certain regions. Some examples are Stuttgart Army Airfield in Germany that no longer has a passenger terminal or any services. It may still be possible (very rare) to catch a Space-A flight into the airfield, but not to leave from that location.

Lages Field Air Base in the Azores is a Portuguese Air Base where the U.S. Air Force is stationed by agreement with the Republic of Portugal. The DoD decided in 2012 to transition from an airbase wing to an airbase group which resulted in a reduction of more than 400 military personnel and associated dependents. This move also reduced the amount of Space-A opportunities. A recent check of the Lages Passenger Terminal Facebook page showed no Space-A flights in the past six months. The Space-A landscape is constantly changing so it is advisable to check with passenger terminals by telephone, by checking their Facebook page, or keeping current through Space-A Facebook groups or websites.

Security Screenings as Space-A Passengers

Generally, all Space-A passengers will undergo a normal security screening similar to the screenings done at commercial airports. This may require passengers to remove any metal items, shoes, coats, and be subject to search of their person or luggage.

Changes to Space-A Rules

The rules and policies constantly change. These changes can range from very minor to major. These changes can pertain to who is eligible to travel Space-A, sign-up procedures, Patriot Express routes or a variety of other Space-A matters. Some changes that occurred in the past include:

- Removing the $10 fee per person to use Space-A
- No longer having to wear a uniform while using Space-A
- Being able to sign-up remotely
- Unaccompanied dependent Space-A travel
- Changing the sign-up duration from 45 days to 60 days for AMC locations

Differences between Command-sponsored and Non-Command Sponsored

Command sponsorship means that the family of the active duty service member is authorized to travel to the overseas assignment and that the government will provide housing, medical care and education for the children. A non-command sponsored dependent is not authorized for travel reimbursement but may decide to travel at their own expense.

The government will not provide housing, the dependent will need to meet country residency requirements and medical care will be on a space available basis.

Manifested

If passengers are selected for a flight, then they are considered manifested for that flight. Passengers can only be manifested for one flight at a time. Until the aircraft leaves the runway, there is always the possibility that something happens and passengers no longer become manifested and lose their seat. Manifested through means that passengers do not have to compete for seats with other passengers at an en route location. For instance, when we took a Space-A flight from Norfolk, Virginia to Roosevelt Roads, Puerto Rico, we were manifested through to Puerto Rico. When the plane landed in Jacksonville, Florida and then later in Guantanamo Bay, Cuba, before arriving in Puerto Rico, we did not have to compete against all the passengers in Florida or Cuba that were trying to get on the flight at those locations.

Alcoholic Beverages

Alcoholic beverages are not served on military aircraft. Any open alcoholic beverages will be confiscated if found. Check with the passenger terminal if you plan to transport containers of sealed alcohol. Passengers may not consume alcoholic beverages from their own supply on a military aircraft. Patriot Express flights may serve alcoholic beverages to passengers of legal age at a cost.

Food on Space-A Flights

Food and soft drinks are free on Patriot Express flights. Space-A passengers, like duty passengers, may purchase beer and wine on Patriot

Express flights. If passengers will be flying on military aircraft (not Patriot Express), then they may have the option to purchase meals from the flight kitchen. Not all passenger terminals will have these meals available and the type of meal provided differs depending on the location. The cost will be nominal and generally consists of a cardboard box containing a sandwich, fruit, snack or dessert, and juice or a soft drink. The meals are distributed while in flight by a crew member. If passengers decide to order a meal, they will make their choice and pay during flight processing. Passengers may bring their own food aboard but no alcoholic beverages. If passengers have a special food requirement, it is best for them to bring their own food onboard. Passenger terminals can restrict the type or amount of food brought on an aircraft but we never witnessed any restrictions.

Changes to the Number of Available Seats

Seat releases can change at any time for a variety of reasons. Some possible reasons include non-working toilets, broken seats, change of destination, hazardous cargo, non-issue of maintenance waiver, or no passenger monitor on board.

Other reasons that are not as obvious include pallets of cargo that can not only affect weight restrictions but how the pallets are configured in the aircraft can restrict safe egress and ingress to the seats. When an aircraft is refueling the amount of fuel can affect the overall weight allowance that in turn will limit the number of available seats. Another possible scenario can occur due to weather as a wet aircraft or wet runway can reduce the number of available seats. If the aircraft issues a seat release on arrival it may change if any of the above issues appear.

For seat increases it could be something as simple as a piece of cargo that cannot make the flight or a leg of the mission is dropped so less fuel is required. Other increases can happen as a maintenance issue is fixed or waivered to be able to take passengers or a new crew member is available to be trained to be a passenger monitor.

Seat Assignments on Military Aircraft

Generally, seats will be first-come, first-served. On some military flights priority for boarding will be given to those in a special category such as medal of honor holders or passengers with the rank of colonel and above and thus they will have a better choice in available seating. We experienced this on one occasion in a C-5 Galaxy where retired colonels and their spouses were allowed to board the aircraft first and then also exited the aircraft before anyone else.

Seat Codes on Flight Schedules

TBD (To Be Determined): The Passenger Terminal is unable to determine the potential number of seats at the current time.

SP (Seats Pending): The Passenger Terminal is working to determine the number of available seats but is still in the process of making the determination once they have certain information such as cargo considerations and mission details.

T (Tentative) or **TSR** (Tentative Seats Released): The Passenger Terminal made a determination on the number of seats based on the current mission and cargo details but there may be other factors that may alter the seat count such as maintenance issues, fuel weight, or weather.

F (Firm): The Passenger Terminal made a seat determination based on all known factors and the seat count should be final. Of course, there is always a chance that even the firm seat count can change before take-off due to last-minute changes.

Space-A Travel for Military Widows or Widowers

Currently, widows and widowers of active duty or retired military personnel are not entitled to Space-A travel aboard DoD aircraft. Changes to the rules are introduced by certain members of Congress periodically but no changes were made with respect to military widows or widowers. For instance, in 2012, the Space Available Act of 2012 was introduced as House Bill 4162 sponsored by Representative Don Young (R-AK) and Senate Bill 2112, sponsored by Senator Mark Begich (D-AK) in an attempt to not only allow military widows and widowers to access Space-A travel but also to expand access to Gray Area retirees and dependents of Guard and Reserve members. These bills did not pass.

Ability to Utilize Space-A Travel when Retired Sponsor is Deceased

Space-A travel is a privilege granted to the service member and does not carry over after death to dependents. The one exception is for dependents of retired uniformed services members who die overseas. In this case, travel is authorized for the purpose of accompanying the remains of the deceased retired member from overseas to the CONUS. Return travel is authorized if accomplished within one year of arrival in the CONUS. Documentation certified by DoD mortuary affairs personnel shall be presented to passenger terminal personnel and shall be in the dependents' possession during travel.

Space-A Flights Only for Active Duty

The primary reason some Space-A flights are restricted to active duty only is that the destination of the particular aircraft does not have a customs agent available to clear non-active duty passengers. Active duty passengers are not required to clear customs but retirees, dependents, or civilians have to go through customs when traveling overseas.

Final Destination Guarantee if Manifested

Passengers will not be removed or "bumped" in favor of another Space-A passenger once they are manifested. But passengers can be removed either at the originating location or even en route to the final destination for other reasons. These reasons can include accommodating Space-Required passengers, mission cargo, or medevac passengers. If passengers do get removed from the plane, they will need to start over using their original date and time of sign-up. The order of selection for removal will begin with the lowest priority passenger with the latest date and time of sign-up as reflected on the manifest.

Flying Space-A with Firearms

Space-A passengers are allowed to bring firearms. The firearms must be declared and turned over to the passenger service agents as soon as the passenger enters the passenger terminal so that the firearms can be secured until the passenger is selected and checked-in for a flight. All weapons must be transported in a locked case or as checked luggage. No more than 11 pounds of ammo can be transported with the weapon. If passengers are attempting to travel to a foreign country their laws may prevent the passenger from being able to take weapons into or through the country in which case the passenger will be prohibited on the flight. Travelers also need to be aware of any local, state, or military installation laws on firearms (and other weapons) before traveling to the passenger terminal.

Defense Transportation Regulation 4500.9-R, Appendix S, contains procedures for transporting firearms and small arms ammunition on DoD aircraft. Host nation restrictions at arrival locations are identified in the Foreign Clearance Guide (FCG). *Air Mobility Command*

Instruction 24-101, Volume 14, Paragraph 32, states that passengers may transport unloaded, un-prohibited firearms/ammunition in or as checked baggage; except when restricted by regulation, law, or FCG. Passengers must declare to a passenger service agent that their firearm is unloaded. Authorization is then granted to allow a passenger to transport personal firearms in their checked baggage. Firearms will be stored in a container appropriate for air transportation.

Medevac Flights

The C-9 Nightingales, which were used exclusively for MEDEVAC flights, started their service in 1968 and were retired in 2005. Currently, the MEDEVAC mission is accomplished by using a variety of wide-bodied aircraft such as the C-17, C-130, and occasionally C-5 aircraft. Removable MEDEVAC litter and ambulatory pallets are used and may be placed by a forklift into the aircraft being used for air evacuation. Their flight schedules are based on need and are no longer on a routine schedule. We once flew on a C-5 from Germany to the U.S. that contained several patients and medical personnel.

Travel to Unaccompanied Tour Areas

Non-command sponsored dependents of active duty uniformed services members serving unaccompanied PCS OCONUS may use Space-A transportation to and from the member's approved overseas tour location, as approved by the installation commander concerned. Travel under this program is not authorized when the sponsor is on TDY/TAD orders. CONUS-CONUS travel is not authorized unless passengers are manifested on an aircraft that is only transiting the en route CONUS location. The uniformed services member must obtain prior written approval for non-command sponsored dependent travel from the installation or unit commander concerned. This documentation will be presented to passenger terminal personnel, stay in the dependent's possession during travel, and remain valid for one round-trip to the sponsor's PCS duty location.

Space-A Travel Restrictions

Passengers cannot use Space-A privileges for personal gain or in connection with business enterprises or employment. They also cannot use Space-A travel to establish a home, to transport dependents to a duty station where they are or will be serving an unaccompanied tour, to transport dependents to a TDY duty station, or when international or theater restrictions prohibit such travel.

Marking Yourself Present for a Space-A Flight

Passengers may mark themselves present for a flight up to 24 hours prior to the scheduled flight.

The Next Step after Sign-Up

On the day passengers would like to travel, they must be "Marked-Present" to be included during the Space-A Roll Call for travel. See a Passenger Service Agent at the Check-In or Customer Service Counter. Passengers may be "Marked-Present" up to 24 hours prior to Roll Call. If passengers fail to get on a flight, they need to ensure they are still listed as present if they plan to try for other flights. Some locations purge their list daily so travelers should ask the passenger terminal about the policy.

Date and Time of Sign-up

Date and Time of Sign-up is the time used to determine the next selected passenger in their category during the Roll Call process. The original date and time of sign-up shall be documented and stay with the passenger until their destination is reached. On reaching their destination, the passenger may again sign-up for Space-A travel to return to their home residence.

Passenger Terminal Phone Numbers

The AMC Travel Resource Page contains a link to a document with current information on all AMC passenger terminals.

Status of Forces Agreement (SOFA)

A status of forces agreement (SOFA) is an agreement between a host country and a foreign nation stationing military forces in that country. SOFAs are often included, along with other types of military agreements, as part of a comprehensive security arrangement. A SOFA does not constitute a security arrangement; it establishes the rights and privileges of foreign personnel present in a host country in support of the larger security arrangement. For example, the U.S. has a SOFA with Germany and South Korea among other countries.

Sometimes a SOFA stamp is placed in person's passport. It is a document or stamp in your passport that shows you are stationed in a country and covered by the Status of Forces Agreement. The SOFA stamp registers the person and identifies them as having protections and rights under the SOFA agreement.

The SOFA may cover issues like entry and exit into the country, tax liabilities, postal services, or employment terms for host-country nationals, but the most contentious issues are civil and criminal jurisdiction over bases and personnel.

Some SOFAs may restrict your eligibility to use the military Exchange or commissary facilities in a country and may govern entry procedures into a country when traveling via Space-A. For example, the Misawa passenger terminal in Japan states that Government of Japan Immigrations are only available Mondays and Tuesdays for Non-SOFA personnel. Non-SOFA travelers upon arrival to Misawa Air Base, Japan will receive a Government of Japan Immigrations Visa which is valid for 90 days. Non-SOFA personnel arriving in Japan on any other day of the week will surrender their passport to a Security Forces Customs & Immigrations representative. While your passport is being held you cannot depart the military installation until Japanese Immigrations places a Visa in your passport.

Dependents, Children, and Infants

Generally, dependents may travel Space-A only when accompanied by their sponsors.

Command-sponsored Dependent Travel

- Travelers are responsible for obtaining all country, theater, and border clearance documentation and having the necessary funds when traveling between theaters.
- A sponsor must obtain verification of command sponsorship in the form of a verification letter signed and dated by their current section or unit commander. Each letter is valid for one round trip from the sponsor's OCONUS permanent duty station.
- Travelers must present a copy of the verification letter to the servicing air passenger terminal for movement and maintain a copy of the letter during travel.
- Travelers may sign up for Space-A travel on or after the date the verification letter is signed by the unit commander; however, travelers will be removed from the Space-A roster upon expiration of travel authorization or after 60 days, whichever occurs first.
- Passenger service agents will accept only verification letters signed by commanders or acting commanders, or orders signed by "By Direction" authority in the case of the Navy and Marine Corps. Squadron section commanders assigned to headquarters may sign verification letters for those sponsors assigned to headquarters billets.

Dependents of Deployed Active Duty Uniformed Services Members.

- Dependents 18 years of age or older of deployed active duty uniformed services members are eligible to travel unaccompanied when the deployment orders indicate the deployment is for 30 consecutive days or more. Dependents are authorized to travel for the duration of the sponsor's deployment. There is no limit on the number of trips. Dependents may sign up for travel no earlier than 10 days before the sponsor's deployment and are eligible to commence travel effective on the first day of the sponsor's deployment.

- Eligible dependents must present to air terminal personnel a verification letter signed by the member's commander verifying the member's length of deployment. The verification letter must remain in the dependent's possession during travel.

- Unfunded Emergency Travel of Dependents Stationed in the CONUS. When funded emergency travel is not authorized for unaccompanied dependents stationed in the CONUS traveling OCONUS, travel may be authorized. The sponsor must obtain verification in the form of a letter signed by the commander or acting commander, or orders signed by "By Direction" authority in the case of the Navy and Marine Corps. Squadron commanders assigned to headquarters may sign verification letters for those sponsors assigned to headquarters billets.

Space-A Travel with Small Children

Most aircraft will have a limited number of infant life preservers known as "infant cots." The infant life preserver model is LPU-6/P and is designed for infants weighing no more than 30 lbs. The infant is commonly referred to as an "in-lap" child and is fewer than two years of age. This is different than the LPU-21 E/P or LPU-37/P model for adults. It is the only life preserver that can be inflated inside the aircraft. The number of infants allowed on a Space-A flight will be limited to the number of available infant cots.

Infant car seats are not mandatory but are highly encouraged. Passengers may use FAA approved Child Restraint Systems (CRS) intended for use in flight based on the following weight and size for children:

- Less than 20 pounds: Use a rear-facing CRS.
- Between 20-40 pounds: Use a forward-facing CRS.
- More than 40 pounds: Use an airplane seatbelt.

A passenger CRS must be government approved and have the following statement attached "This restraint is certified for use in motor vehicles and aircraft." A CRS or fold up type strollers will not count against the passenger's normal baggage allowance. Further information can be found in *Air Mobility Command Instruction 24-101, Volume 14.*

Per the Transportation Security Administration (TSA), formula, breast milk, and juice are allowed in reasonable quantities in carry-on bags. Remove these items from your carry-on bag to be screened separately from the rest of your belongings. You do not need to travel with your child to bring breast milk. Of course, the final decision rests with the TSA officer or screening personnel whether an item is allowed through the checkpoint. Most AMC aircraft will have water available on the flight so powder formula may also be an option to consider as well as certain milk products that do not require refrigeration.

If ordering a meal to bring on the Space-A flight, ask the passenger terminal agent if cheese or peanut butter and jelly sandwiches are an available option. Also, consider bringing snacks that your small child enjoys.

If traveling without a sponsor then each child (regardless of age) needs to be included on a dependent travel memo. Also, children age 10 and over are required to have an ID card for Space-A travel. For children under 10 years of age (without ID cards), passengers may use passports, or the child's DoD ID number which can be retrieved from the MilConnect website.

Since some military aircraft types can be extremely cold during the flight, ensure that children are adequately dressed. Even toddlers are required to wear solid shoes as no open-toed footwear or sandals are allowed on military aircraft.

Every passenger, including children and infants, is required to have an assigned seat. If your group includes two adults, two small children and one infant for a total of five but only four seats are available, your entire group will not be allowed on the flight.

U.S. Customs and Border Protection (CBP) strongly recommends that unless the child is accompanied by both parents, the adult have a note from the child's other parent (or, in the case of a child traveling with grandparents, uncles or aunts, sisters or brothers, friends, or in groups, a note signed by both parents) stating "I acknowledge that my wife/husband/etc. is traveling out of the country with my son/daughter/group. He/She/They has/have my permission." Adults traveling with children should also be aware that, while the U.S. does not require this documentation, other countries may have a requirement and failure to produce notarized permission letters and/or birth certificates could result in travelers being refused entry (Canada has very strict requirements in this regard).

Required Dependent Documentation without an ID Card and Less than 10 Years Old

Dependents without an ID card and less than 10 years old must have proof of age, i.e. birth certificate, passport, or other Government provided document. A dependent's DoD ID number can be retrieved from the MilConnect website.

Transportation of Minors

Minors must be accompanied by a parent or legal guardian at all times when traveling in a Space-A status on DoD aircraft. A power of attorney or another non-judicial document that has not been issued or approved by a court transferring legal responsibility for the minor will not be accepted to satisfy this requirement.

Space-A Travel While Pregnant

Pregnant women up to the 34th week of gestation may be transported unless medically inadvisable. Women less than 6 weeks postpartum and infants under 6 weeks old may be accepted for transportation if considered medically sound and so certified in writing by a responsible medical officer or civilian physician. In a medical emergency, a pregnant woman of more than 34 weeks or a child younger than six weeks and the mother will be flown on a medical evacuation (MEDEVAC) flight as patients.

Unaccompanied Command-Sponsored Dependent Space-A Travel of a Uniformed Service Member

Command-sponsored dependents of a uniformed service member may utilize Space-A travel unaccompanied if they are 18 years of age or older. However, the intent of this program is to afford command sponsored dependents relief from their overseas duty location. Travel is authorized Overseas-CONUS, CONUS-Overseas, and Overseas-Overseas within the same theater. Once the dependent lands in the CONUS, they are no longer authorized to travel Space-A to another destination unless they are manifested on an aircraft that is only transiting the en route CONUS location.

Unaccompanied Non-Command-Sponsored Dependent Space-A Travel

Non-command sponsored dependents make utilize Space-A travel unaccompanied if they are 18 years or older. Travel is authorized to the sponsor's unaccompanied permanent PCS location. Travel is not authorized to meet up at another location. Travel under this program is not authorized when the sponsor is on TDY/TAD orders. Travel is authorized CONUS-Overseas, Overseas-CONUS, and Overseas-Overseas. Once the dependent lands in the CONUS, they are no longer authorized to travel Space-A to another destination. CONUS-CONUS travel is not authorized unless they are manifested on an aircraft that is only transiting the en route CONUS location.

Unaccompanied Space-A Travel if Sponsor is Deployed

Unaccompanied dependents of deployed uniformed service members, when the deployment orders indicate the deployment is between 30 and 365 consecutive days, are authorized to travel Space-A unaccompanied in Category IV. If the deployment period exceeds 365 consecutive days, the unaccompanied dependents are authorized Category III travel. However, travelers will only be eligible to move in this category after every other Category 3 member has been selected.

Space-A Travel with Family Members

Except for EML and emergency travel, family members must be accompanied by the sponsor to fly Space-A with limited exception. Family members may travel to/from and between overseas locations and within the Continental United States (CONUS) depending on the situation. Dependents of active duty members may travel within the CONUS when accompanying their sponsor on emergency leave. Dependents may accompany the sponsor on permissive house-hunting trips incident to a permanent change of station (PCS). Command sponsored dependents stationed overseas are allowed unaccompanied travel to, from, and within the overseas theater (in addition to environmental morale leave previously authorized). Travel restrictions may apply to certain overseas areas as determined by the unified commander. Unaccompanied dependents must have documentation signed by their sponsor's commander verifying command sponsorship during their travel and shown to passenger terminal personnel. This document is only valid for one round-trip from the sponsor's duty location. Family members under 18 years of age must be accompanied by an eligible parent or legal guardian. These changes do not affect the assignment categories for Space-A travel.

Disabilities

Passenger service personnel and aircraft crewmembers may provide assistance in boarding, seating, and deplaning a disabled passenger. Transportation may be disapproved by the chief of the passenger travel section or the aircraft commander if there is an unacceptable risk to the safety or health of the disabled passenger or other passengers or crew, or if operational necessity, equipment, or manpower limitations preclude accepting a disabled passenger, service animal, or mobility assistance device. The aircraft commander is the final approval authority on all matters relating to flight safety.

Space-A Travel as a Disabled Veteran with a Retiree Card (DD Form 2)

A disabled veteran who is also retired with a DD Form 2 may utilize Space-A travel. However, travelers need to be aware of certain restrictions. If travelers require motorized assistance to move around, the current allowance is for mobility assistance equipment that shall not exceed 100 lbs. in weight.

Space-A Travel as a Disabled Veteran or 100% Disabled Veteran but not Retired

With the extending of eligibility, veterans with a permanent service-connected disability rated as total are now able to compete for travel in Space-A Category VI, traveling in the Continental United States (CONUS) or directly between the CONUS and Alaska, Hawaii, Puerto Rico, the U.S. Virgin Islands, Guam, and American Samoa (Guam and American Samoa travelers may transit Hawaii or Alaska); or traveling within Alaska, Hawaii, Puerto Rico, or the U.S. Virgin Islands.

Having a Friend or Relative Accompany a Disabled Retiree or Dependent (Other Than 100% Disabled Veteran) During Space-A Travel

The only persons permitted to accompany the traveler are the spouse, dependents or other persons eligible for Space-A travel. Every effort shall be made to transport passengers with disabilities who are otherwise eligible to travel. In some instances, however not required, passenger service personnel and crew members may provide assistance in boarding, seating, and deplaning passengers with special needs. Current Space-A privileges do not extend to 100% disabled veteran's spouse or dependents.

Space-A Travel on a Military Aircraft with a Seatbelt Extender

Space-A passengers must be able to secure themselves in military aircraft without the use of a seatbelt extender. These passengers may not be able to fly on certain military aircraft that have conventional airline seats such as the C-5, C-17 or some smaller military aircraft. If the passenger can secure themselves in an aircraft that does not utilize standard aircraft seats such as a C-130 or other aircraft where web seats are used, they will be able to travel.

Luggage

Space-A travelers may generally check two pieces of luggage at 70 pounds each per person. Checked baggage may not exceed 62 linear inches (length plus width plus height). Carry-on baggage must fit under the seat and may not exceed 45 linear inches (length plus width plus height.) Each passenger is permitted to hand-carry one article (small luggage, garment bags, backpack, etc.) and one personal item (cosmetic case, purse, briefcase, small boxes, packages, etc.) for storage in the passenger cabin area. Family members traveling together may pool their baggage allowance as long as the total does not exceed the total allowance. Smaller type aircraft have restrictions (C-12, C-21, UC-35 aircraft have a 30 pounds total baggage limitation. Navy C-40 & C-9's are restricted to two bags at 50 pounds total). To maximize seat availability, terminal personnel may further restrict passenger baggage allowances.

Paying for Excess Baggage on Space-A Flights

Only duty status passengers, Space-Required, may pay for excess baggage. Space-A passengers are not authorized excess baggage.

Baggage Recommendations

Travel light and take only essential items. Do not place valuables, medicine, or important documents in checked baggage. Be sure your name and current address are on and inside your bags. AMC terminals have baggage ID tags available for your use. It is also advisable to place a copy of your leave/EML paperwork inside your checked baggage.

Documentation, Registers, and Virtual Roll Call

The traveler must possess a valid form of a U.S. government identification card during travel. All passengers must have in their possession an official identification card issued by a DoD Component, federal, state, or local government authority. Additionally, overseas travelers may be required to carry documents such as passports, immunization records, and visas. Passengers lacking proper identification and other documents may be denied transportation.

Specific required documentation must be presented to the passenger terminal personnel or other appropriate authority when requested, and includes the following:

Uniformed services members on active duty (including National Guard and Reserve Component on active duty in excess of 30 days or Active Guard Reserve), U.S. Public Health Service nurses, National Oceanic and Atmospheric Administration Commissioned Officer Corps officers, and cadets and midshipmen of the U.S. Military Academies must have:

- A common access card (CAC).
- A valid leave authorization or other documentation required by the Military Service.
- A DD Form 1173, "Uniformed Services Identification and Privilege Card," for any dependents accompanying the member.

Reserve Component members on active duty for 30 days or fewer (includes National Guard and Reserves) must have:

- A CAC or DD Form 2S (RES), "Armed Forces of the United States – Geneva Conventions Identification Card (Reserve)

(Green)."
- Orders placing the Reservist on active duty.

Retired uniformed services members must have:

- A DD Form 2S (RET), "United States Uniformed Services Identification Card (Retired) (Blue)."
- A DD Form 1173 for any dependents accompanying the sponsor.

Authorized Reserve Component members (including the remainder of the Ready Reserve not accounted for above, as well as the Standby Reserve standby active status list) must have:

- A CAC.
- A DD Form 1853.

Retired Reservists under the age of 60, but entitled to retired pay at age 60 ("gray area retirees") must have a DD Form 2S (RESRET), "United States Uniformed Services Identification Card (Reserve) (Retired)." Notice of retirement eligibility is not required.

Dual-uniformed services members with dependent children, when the non-sponsor military parent or step-parent accompanies his or her dependent minor children on DoD aircraft, must have:

- A CAC.
- A valid DD Form 1173.
- Written approval from the dependent children's sponsor, as identified in the Defense Enrollment Eligibility Reporting System.

EML travelers must have:

- A CAC.
- A valid EML authorization.
- A DD Form 1173 for any dependents accompanying the uniformed services member.

ROTC members, nuclear power officer candidates (NUPOCs), and Civil Engineer Corps (CEC) members must have a DD Form 1853.

Dependents of uniformed services members who are under the age of 10 and traveling without a DD Form 1173 must travel with the sponsor or eligible parent. For children under 10 years of age (without ID cards), passengers may use passports, or the child's DoD ID number which can be retrieved from the MilConnect website.

Medal of Honor recipients and dependents of Medal of Honor recipients, when accompanied by their sponsor, must have a DD Form 1173.

There are several other less used categories that can be found in DoD Instruction 4515.13. This includes foreign exchange service officers, American Samoan veterans, personnel assigned to Diego Garcia or Guantanamo Bay or certain employees of the American Red Cross, USO, and USS when they provide direct support to the DoD.

Registers and Sign-Up Procedures

Each installation from which Space-A transportation is offered will establish a single Space-A register. All passengers accepted for airlift from that location must have been selected from the register's roll. Maintenance of the register is the responsibility of the AMC passenger activity, where established. To compete for Space-A travel, eligible personnel must present all required documentation and sign up on the Space-A roster either in person or remotely, where such capability exists.

The original date and time of sign-up will be documented and remain with the traveler until movement to their declared final destination is complete, their leave terminates, or a maximum of 60 days has passed, whichever occurs first. The Combatant Commander may further restrict this time limit for assigned personnel. Those registered are not required to accept any seat offered and failure to accept an offered seat will not jeopardize a passenger's position on the space available register. Passengers dropped from the register may sign up again in their respective categories and will be provided a new date and time of sign-up.

Virtual Roll Call

There are a few passenger terminals that provide a service called Virtual Roll Call (VRC) for Space-A flights. This is a relatively new system and travelers have reported a variety of results using VRC. We never used this system as we prefer to check the passenger terminal Facebook site, call the passenger terminal and speak with a representative for the latest information and be physically present to ensure we are properly signed in and available for roll call. The idea behind VRC is that you do not need to be present at the terminal during roll call. Even with VRC, you need to go to the passenger terminal within 24 hours of roll call, mark yourself present, and ensure your email address on file is correct. What is supposed to happen is that approximately one hour before roll call, you should receive a roll call notification email. If you do not respond to the email, you are no longer eligible for that particular Space-A flight. If you respond, you will receive one of two emails. Either you will receive a flight selection email and check your bags and prepare for the flight or you will receive a non-selection email. Personally, I would not take the chance that the email does not get sent out promptly or for some reason, you do not receive the email (delay, no signal, etc.)

Environmental Morale Leave (EML) Travel

EML stands for Environmental and Morale Leave. Typically, only unfunded EML travel is authorized for use in the Space-A program. Passengers traveling in the EML status are given a higher priority than those traveling on ordinary leave.

Unfunded Environmental Morale Leave (EML) Travel

Environmental and Morale Leave is leave authorized at an overseas installation where adverse environmental conditions require special arrangements for leave in desirable places at periodic intervals.

The Combatant Commander or designee may designate authorized EML duty locations and destinations in their area of responsibility. Dependents under 18 years of age traveling under EML orders must be accompanied by an EML-eligible parent or legal guardian who is traveling in an EML status. Dependents 18 years of age or older may travel unaccompanied but may also require a separate command sponsored Space-A letter for travel.

Unfunded EML travelers may travel in Category II status to only one EML destination for each set of EML orders. This does not preclude several approved destinations being included in a single set of EML orders, as long as procedures are in effect to ensure that the individual is provided Category II status only for travel to and from the first authorized EML destination actually reached. Subsequent Space-A travel (e.g., from the EML destination to a third location and return, or from the third location to another EML location) may be provided only in Category III status.

Reservist and Guard Members

Reserve/Guard members with a valid Common Access Card (CAC) and the DD Form 1853 may fly to, from, and between Alaska, Hawaii, Puerto Rico, the Virgin Islands, Guam, American Samoa, and the Continental United States (CONUS). Dependents are not authorized to travel. However, when on active duty for more than 30 consecutive days and in a leave status, members and their dependents may fly to overseas locations where AMC has operating flights.

Space-A Travel as a Retired Reservist with Dependents

Dependents can travel with retired sponsors if their sponsor carries a DD Form 2 (Blue retired ID card), not a DD Form 2 (Red). When carrying a "Red" card, only the sponsor can travel Space-A.

Animals

Space-A passengers may not travel with a pet. DoD has reserved pet shipments for passengers in Permanent Change of Station (PCS) status. But service animals may fly with a traveler using Space-A with proper documentation.

Service Animals Rules

Transportation of a service animal in the cabin or cargo hold is authorized without charge when accompanying a passenger who is disabled. DoD personnel will make every effort to ensure individuals with disabilities are not separated from their service animals. An animal's weight and size, as well as USDA and foreign country restrictions, may limit the transport of a service animal within the cabin or cargo hold.

Emotional Support Animals (ESAs)/Psychiatric Support Animals Rules

Passengers must provide proper documentation in order to travel with an emotional support or psychiatric service animal. Documentation may be no older than one year from the date of the passenger's initial scheduled flight and must be on the letterhead of a licensed mental health professional (psychiatrist, psychologist, or licensed clinical social worker). ESA animals will only travel in the cabin with the passenger.

Additional Information Concerning Both Service Animals and ESAs

Service Animals (if in cabin) and ESAs must sit on the customer's lap, or at their feet without protruding into the aisle or encroach on the other passengers. Proper sanitation is the responsibility of the traveler and must be maintained at all times. Passenger service personnel and aircrew members are not required to provide care or food for a service/emotional support animal or provide a special location for the animal's hygiene needs. Animals may be removed from the premises if the handler cannot control the animal or the animal poses a threat to the health or safety of other passengers or passenger service personnel. Transportation of service animals and ESAs are subject to country quarantine procedures. When it is necessary to detain a service animal/ESA pending a determination of admissibility, the traveler will provide detention facilities that are satisfactory to the quarantine officer. The passenger will bear the expense of such detention, including necessary examinations, vaccinations, and other expenses incurred. For additional information, see the HQ AMC Pet Brochure dated April 2018 or the AMC Pet Travel information page.

Retirees

Retired service members with a DD Form 2 (Blue) identification card may fly anywhere AMC has operating flights, including the Continental United States.

Space-A Travel as a Retiree Traveling from Overseas on a Passport into CONUS

When traveling on a passport, all family members, retired uniform service, reserve, and others may return to the CONUS only through authorized ports of entry where customs and immigration clearance is available. Active duty passengers who do not require immigration clearance have more reentry options available. This is why you will sometimes see flights that will not accept other than active duty passengers. While you may depart the CONUS literally from any military airfield, reentry locations for passport holders are limited due to customs and immigration clearance requirements.

Space-A Travel as a Gray Area Retiree

A gray area retiree with a pink ID card (Reservist who is normally eligible for retirement pay at 60 years of age but not fully retired with a blue ID card), can fly Space-A only within the CONUS and directly between the CONUS and Alaska, Hawaii, Puerto Rico, the US Virgin Islands, Guam, and American Samoa (Guam and American Samoa travelers may transit Hawaii or Alaska); or traveling within Alaska, Hawaii, Puerto Rico or the Virgin Islands. Gray area dependents are not authorized to fly Space-A until the gray area retiree has fully retired and has the blue-uniformed services ID card. Once the gray area retiree has the blue-uniformed services ID card then they and their accompanied dependents can use Space-A to travel anywhere Space-A is allowed. Some reservists may obtain their retiree status before the age of 60 due to a law change in 2008.

Exchanges and Commissaries Overseas

The utilization of AAFES Exchange stores overseas depends on the traveler's status and the specific location. For the exact answer, view the Overseas Customer page on the Exchange website that can be found at: www.aafes.com/exchange-stores/overseas.

Exchange privileges in overseas areas are at the discretion of the host country and are not automatic. The Exchange does not determine shopping privileges or access to duty-free goods. Overseas commanders, in accordance with the host countries and U.S. international agreements, determine who will be extended shopping privileges.

For instance, in Germany active duty U.S. military, DoD civilians and dependents are eligible to access AAFES Exchange stores if assigned or TDY to Germany. If those same people are on leave from another country or area, then only personnel stationed in Europe and North Africa are eligible. Retired U.S. military and dependents visiting from the U.S. or residing in Germany must be an ordinary resident or be visiting Germany for a period of 30 days or more. Rationed items may not be purchased. All purchases are subject to the payment of a fixed-rate tax to German customs. In Greece, retired military visiting from the U.S. are not eligible. If you are denied access, you may find opportunities at other base locations such as shoppettes or locally-run stores.

Accessing Commissaries Located Outside the U.S.

Commissary privileges overseas are covered under Status of Forces Agreements (SOFA), Visiting Forces agreements, treaties, etc. Since products sold in overseas commissaries pass across international borders and are subject to customs, duty, and tax-free considerations, there may be shopping restrictions. These restrictions are to protect the interest of the host nation and to resolve legal, customs, and tax issues. The agreements allow for some exemptions from host nation tax laws, but nonetheless, the privilege is substantially restricted and will vary from country to country. These agreements are negotiated between the Military Services, the U.S. State Department, and the host nation. Some countries allow exemptions from host nation tax laws; others require the payment of taxes, fees, or tariffs. Many do not allow the purchase of rationed items for visitors.

Other countries have minimum stay requirements to be eligible, but the privilege is restricted for military personnel, retired, DoD civilians, DoD contractors and their family members. In addition, commissary privileges for DoD contractors who are stationed or TDY overseas are restrictive and not automatic.

The Military Services, installation commanders, and the Defense Commissary Agency must enforce and cannot grant exceptions to the agreements. DoD civilians and DoD contractors in TDY status unless on emergency evacuation orders to the U.S. from an overseas area not authorized commissary privileges. DoD civilians not on official duty from the U.S. to overseas are not entitled to overseas commissary privileges.

Patriot Express

The Patriot Express, also known as a Rotator, Freedom Bird or simply Pat-Ex, is a DoD commercial charter flight. The DoD normally charters with commercial airlines when they expect a certain route is needed on a regular basis to fly military passengers and their dependents and doing so will be more economical than using military aircraft or existing commercial aircraft. This means that there will be several, if not all, passengers on a Patriot Express flight that are flying on a Space-Required rather than Space-A basis. An example of Space-Required is when a service member is assigned to Germany and his family is command sponsored so they then use the Patriot Express flight to move to Germany to begin their new assignment. After all the official passengers are manifested on the Patriot Express flight, any remaining seats will be made available to Space-A travelers based on the normal Space-A eligibility and category procedures. Seats will be assigned based on availability with the exception of distinguished visitor (DV) passengers who will normally sit in the first two rows of the aircraft.

The sign-up process for Patriot Express is the same as for normal Space-A travel. There is a cost to fly Patriot Express flights. The cost is per passenger, regardless of age, and covers the head tax and inspection fees. As some passenger terminals may not have a credit card reader, you will want to have cash to cover this cost. The cost varies depending on your flight route but ensure you have at least $33 per person on hand. Passenger terminals will normally post their Patriot Express flights on a monthly schedule but the seat availability will not be posted any earlier than 72 hours in advance.

Although Patriot Express flights operate on a fairly consistent schedule, weather or maintenance issues can interfere with the schedule. Just because a Patriot Express flight exists does not mean that it cannot be canceled. For instance, the Patriot Express flights that used to go to Roosevelt Roads, Puerto Rico no longer exists as the former Navy base was transferred and is now a public-use airport. Some current Patriot Express flights include Seattle International Airport (SeaTac) in Seattle, Washington State to Japan and Guam; Baltimore Washington International (BWI) Airport outside Baltimore, Maryland to Germany, Greenland, New Jersey and Turkey; Naval Station Norfolk in Virginia to Florida, Cuba, Spain, Greece and Bahrain; and Travis Air Force Base in California to Hawaii.

Since there may be both Space-Required and Space-A passengers on a Patriot Express flight, there will be two separate roll calls. Given the possible commotion and number of travelers waiting for a Patriot Express flight, ensure that you hear your name being called and do not repeat the mistake we once made during a Patriot Express roll call where the passenger terminal representative mispronounced our name and we missed our opportunity. Also, it may be worthwhile to remain at the passenger terminal until all passengers are on the flight as sometimes a few more seats become available at the last moment.

Space-A Military Aircraft

Our primary Space-A experience had our family flying in C-5 or C-17 aircraft. On occasion, there may be an opportunity to fly Space-A in less typical aircraft like the Navy P-3 Orion that I took as a cadet flying out of Hawaii. Below are the most common types of military aircraft that have Space-A seats.

C-5 Galaxy. This is a large military transport aircraft originally made by Lockheed and now made by Lockheed Martin that has a separate area away from the cargo hold that contains airline passenger seats. There will be a long internal ladder or external stairs to access the plane. These are my personal favorite aircraft for flying Space-A but they have an abundant amount of maintenance issues and we experienced several delays attempting to use them for Space-A travel. Twenty passengers and above requires an open pallet position for passenger baggage. The C-5 passenger compartment is accessible using either the 36-step C-5 staircase truck or when the C-5 staircase truck is not available, the 15-step wide body staircase truck and the 14-step interior ladder.

C-17 Globemaster III. This is a large military transport aircraft originally from McDonnell Douglas and later Boeing. The C-17 commonly performs tactical and strategic airlift missions, transporting troops and cargo throughout the world. Generally, you will be sitting in a cargo netting type seat unless you have available space on the floor of the aircraft where you may be able to stretch out after take-off. The aircraft floor can get cold so you should have a sleeping bag, air mattress, or yoga pad to stay comfortable. Forty passengers and above requires an additional crew member.

C-20 Gulfstream. This is the military version of a business jet produced by Gulfstream Aerospace with the original version configured for 14 passengers and five crew.

C-21 Learjet. This is a military transport aircraft manufactured by Learjet with a cabin arranged for 6-8 passengers.

C-37A Gulfstream. This is a long-range, jet aircraft that flies up to Mach 0.885, up to 51,000 feet and has a 6,500 nautical mile range. It normally has a crew of four and up to 14 passengers.

C-38A Courier. This is a twin-engine jet manufactured by Israel Aerospace Industries for Gulfstream. It has a crew of two and 6-9 passengers.

C-40A Clipper. This plane is a military version of the Boeing 737-700C. It has a crew of six and can carry either 121 passengers or eight pallets of cargo, or a combination of both.

C-130 Hercules. This plane is an American four-engine turboprop military transport aircraft from Lockheed Martin. It is the longest continuously produced military aircraft. It has a crew of five and can carry 92 passengers or six pallets. Normally Space-A passengers will sit on the sidewall web seats and use a porta-potty type restroom.

KC-10A Extender. This Boeing plane is an aerial refueling tanker aircraft that is a military version of the three-engine DC-10 airliner. It can be configured for a total personnel capacity of 80 crew and support personnel. In an all-cargo configuration, it can accommodate 25-27 pallets. Forty passengers and above requires an additional crew member and greater than ten passengers requires an open pallet position for passenger baggage. The KC-10 utilizes the 24-step wide body staircase truck to board and disembark.

KC-135 Stratotanker. This plane is a military aerial refueling aircraft. It was developed from the Boeing 367-80 prototype. This plane has 3-4 crew and up to 80 passengers. If there are more than ten passengers, there is a requirement for an additional crew member.

Personal Space-A Trips

In order to provide the reader with some examples of how Space-A travel can actually work, I will cover some of my past Space-A adventures. In the forward to the book, I mentioned my first Space-A trip which was as an ROTC cadet in the late 1980s. The trip from Washington State to Hawaii was flawless. Unfortunately, my return trip would prove much more problematic. After spending a few days on the sunny beaches and enjoying the constant warm Hawaii sunshine, it was time to return home. I soon discovered that trips back to the mainland were not as plentiful as the trips to the island. This could just have been because of my poor timing. After trying unsuccessfully for three days, I decided to take whatever flight was going to get me back to the CONUS. Luckily for me there were a couple of seats in a Navy P-3 Orion four-engine turboprop anti-submarine and maritime surveillance aircraft that was going to a base in Illinois. It was quite the experience as it was a relatively small aircraft. When I landed in the remote base, I asked the terminal staff how I could get to Washington State. They just replied that there was a civilian airfield on the other side of the runway. Just then I noticed another aircraft outside the terminal window and asked where it was going. I was told the plane belonged to the Air Guard and was flying to California. So, I quickly managed to jump on that aircraft and fly to an unknown location somewhere in California as that would take me closer to my goal of reaching Washington State.

When I landed in California I asked about Space-A flights and was told that the base where we landed did not have regularly scheduled Space-A flights. But one of the navigators gave me a ride to a bus stop where I waited by myself at 3 am until the first scheduled bus could take me to the nearest commercial airport. Once at the commercial airport, I inquired about getting a commercial flight back to Washington State. At that time, I learned that Travis Air Force base was relatively nearby and so took some additional public transportation to the base. I got really lucky when I arrived as there was a plane that was getting ready to return to McChord Air Force Base in Washington State. But after all passengers got on the plane, we had to deplane as they were experiencing mechanical issues. After about five hours we finally took off.

That trip taught me that Space-A travel is never guaranteed, you need to be ready to use commercial transportation options if you are on a schedule, and being flexible is a key asset. After that exhausting Space-A adventure, my next trip did not materialize until much later when I would be married with a family.

Puerto Rico

While on active duty with the Army stationed at Fort Bragg, North Carolina in 2001, I learned about Space-A trips that went to Puerto Rico. I thought attempting to fly Space-A to Puerto Rico might be a good idea as Puerto Rico is a U.S. territory and would be easier to manage than a long-distance European or Asian country destination. Also, if there were any issues, commercial flights back to the U.S. would be relatively less costly. I learned that flights regularly left from Norfolk, Virginia which was only about a 3.5-hour drive from Fort Bragg. My child and I had no issues getting on the plane going to Puerto Rico. But we soon learned that it would not be a 5.5-hour direct flight to Puerto Rico but the plane was scheduled to make stops in Jacksonville, Florida, and Guantanamo Bay, Cuba. The Jacksonville stop was uneventful, but when we stopped in Guantanamo Bay, we were ushered off the plane and told to remain in a waiting area until the plane was ready to leave and that we were not allowed to leave the waiting room area under any circumstance. The tone of everyone in Guantanamo was much more intense than at any other passenger terminal. When we finally landed in Roosevelt Road, Puerto Rico we learned that the passenger terminal was located on the other side of the base. Fortunately, most Space-A travelers are friendly and helpful and we were able to obtain a ride in a minivan that someone had procured to the other side of the base that contained a Navy Lodge.

The next morning, we had a representative from the local Enterprise Rent-A-Car pick us up from the Navy Lodge and take us to our rental car. We had a great time exploring Old San Juan and the El Yunque National Forest, the only tropical rainforest in the National U.S. Forest System. We would call and visit the passenger terminal on Roosevelt Roads every day but learned that there were no flights returning to the east coast of the U.S. After a few days we were getting a bit desperate and while in the terminal saw a propeller plane that did not appear on the schedule. When I asked about the plane, I was told that the plane just came from South America and was only stopping to refuel and then was going to New Jersey. This was the best news we heard in the past few days and luckily, we managed to get on the plane along with another couple that were also trying to get back home. We learned the other passengers were both in the U.S. Public Health Service Commissioned Corps which is the uniformed personnel system of the U.S. Public Health Service and were eligible to use Space-A. We were able to leave our rental car at the terminal and place the keys in a drop box nearby.

When we landed, we found out we were in Joint Base McGuire-Dix-Lakehurst, New Jersey. A member of the flight crew was kind enough to offer us a ride to the nearest local metro station which we then used to travel to the 30th Street Station, the main train station in Philadelphia. From Philadelphia, we took two Greyhound buses to Norfolk and then a shared taxi back to our vehicle in the long-term parking lot. That trip further illustrated the need for flexibility, the kindness of fellow Space-A travelers and flight crews, and the potential need for commercial transportation options to finish your Space-A journey.

Puerto Rico

After the successful two-person Space-A trip to Puerto Rico in 2001, we decided to try again in 2004 but with the whole family that included the four of us. Again, we left Norfolk, Virginia but this time we were able to take a Patriot Express flight direct to Roosevelt Roads, Puerto Rico. The Patriot Express or Rotator is a DoD contracted commercial charter flight, so we flew in a civilian aircraft. Since we were now a bit familiar with the location, we were able to expand our travel destinations to include visiting Vieques, an island about eight miles from mainland Puerto Rico, using a ferry that departed from Fajardo. Our return flight was surprisingly uneventful as we simply used the scheduled Patriot Express for our return to Norfolk. Given how uncomplicated this family Space-A adventure was, we decided to try again but with our sights set for adventures further afield.

Spain

As we were living in the Washington DC area, we determined that our best options for Space-A travel included Norfolk, Virginia; Joint Base Andrews, Maryland; Baltimore International Airport, Maryland; or Dover Air Force Base, Delaware. Our goal was to travel to Europe and the two primary destinations were Ramstein Air Base in southwestern Germany or Naval Station Rota in Spain. After researching potential flights, we calculated that our best option would be to attempt to use Space-A out of Dover as they had several listed flights going to both Germany and Spain. We were able to fly on a C-5 Galaxy aircraft which is the largest aircraft in the Air Force inventory. Rather than sit in cargo netting seats in the main lower deck of the aircraft, we sat in comfortable seats in the upper deck.

As it was our first time in Rota, we decided to limit our exploration to the local city of Rota and the Naval Station. Rota is a pleasant, small Spanish resort town with several beaches and a long promenade. The

Naval Station had the normal military facilities like an exchange, movie theater, and commissary, but also had a local Spanish restaurant on the base with delicious, inexpensive meals. We were able to walk around with no difficulties. We also were able to get some great information from the base MWR office and exchange funds at the local finance office. We stayed at the Navy Lodge. We managed to get another C-5 aircraft flight back to Dover after having to wait a few days because of mechanical issues that required parts to be flown in. We gained a lot of knowledge of the facilities on base and the local area which helped us plan future travels and to broaden our upcoming experiences.

Germany and England

The following year in 2006 we decided that we would try another Space-A trip but this time attempt to visit Germany. We went back to Dover Air Force Base as they had several flights listed to Germany. We were fortunate again and were able to get on a flight that went to Ramstein Air Base. After we landed in Ramstein Air Base, we were able to obtain lodging on base in one of the several lodging facilities located throughout the base. We learned to check out the flight schedules once we landed to see if there were any exciting available opportunities. We were glad we checked as we learned about a flight to Royal Air Force Mildenhall in Suffolk, England leaving the next day.

After a good night's sleep, we managed to get on the flight to Mildenhall and ended up in England. We obtained lodging on base at an Air Force Inn and found out that there was a free early morning bus that would go to Heathrow Airport. Once at Heathrow we took the tube (subway) into the heart of London. After visiting London for a few days, we reserved seats on a night bus to Paris that used a ferry to get over the English Channel. We discovered that the bus finished its journey at the Gare du Nord train station so we found a local hotel and explored the sights of Paris. Obtaining an all-day subway pass and using the train station lockers proved helpful. When we were finished with

Paris, we took a train back to Ramstein, shared a taxi bus to get back on base and got a quick flight back to Dover. Again, flexibility was key on this trip as it allowed us to visit countries that we had no expectations to visit before we started our trip.

Spain

In 2007 my wife was deployed to Kuwait and I attempted to see if I could actually travel to Kuwait using Space-A. Unfortunately, there was no Space-A availability to Kuwait even though there were several military flights in and out of that region. Looking at the available flights, I determined that Space-A travel to Germany or Spain would be the most likely route and decided to travel with my two children. After only a day's wait, we managed to snag a flight back to Rota, Spain. It was much easier to navigate the base as it was our second visit. The rules kept changing as to what facilities were available for use. For instance, on our first visit, we were able to use the dining facility with the children but were not provided that opportunity on this trip. We did learn through their MWR office that there was a regional bus terminal right outside the main gate. We decided to take a regional bus to the town of Tarifa which is located at the southernmost end of the Iberian Peninsula and known as the world's most popular destination for wind sports. It is also a location where you can take a quick ferry south across the Strait of Gibraltar to Tangier, Morocco in Northern Africa. After a two-hour bus ride, we were able to explore the port town of Tarifa and then catch a return bus back to Rota.

While attempting to leave Rota, the base experienced an electrical shut-down which affected the airport and delayed all flights by several hours. Unfortunately, the delay caused our flight to be postponed by one day. There was another flight the same day but it was going to New Jersey rather than to Delaware and was also canceled. Eventually we were able to fly out the next day. This was another learning lesson about Space-A travel where you will need to make decisions based on constantly changing information. You will face decisions such as whether to take a fairly certain flight going back to the U.S. but not to your final destination or to wait and attempt to catch your optimal flight in the future which may get canceled or postponed. There are no guarantees with Space-A travel.

Spain

Next year in 2008 it was difficult to get the entire family interested in another Space-A trip so just my daughter and I took a short trip back to Rota, Spain. Given our previous experience, we knew that we had a good opportunity to make the entire trip last under one week. We were able to get another quick flight from Dover, Delaware to Rota. For this trip we did our standard walk around Rota but also took a ferry from Rota to Cadiz across the Bay of Cadiz and were able to explore the fascinating city. Cadiz is one of the oldest continuously inhabited cities in Western Europe. We were lucky and managed to obtain a quick fight back to the U.S. and kept our entire trip under one week. After taking multiple Space-A trips, you will gain a better understanding of the process and become more efficient in your traveling itinerary. Also, by visiting the same location, you will gain expertise that will allow you to quickly take care of any logistical issues and just focus on exploring and enjoying your experiences.

Spain

In 2009 some members of the family were starting to get tired of the travels to Spain but our philosophy was that we would take whatever Space-A opportunities were available rather than spend days at a passenger terminal hoping for a specific destination that might never materialize while underutilizing vacation days or leave. So once again, we ended up in Rota, Spain. But for this trip we decided to rent a car on base so we could more readily explore the area. Getting a rental car helped us to visit some interesting places like Gibraltar, Tarifa, Seville, and Tangier. The drive to Gibraltar only took about two hours. Gibraltar is actually a British Overseas Territory and we had to use British Pounds as currency when we entered Gibraltar. The area is less than three square miles so it was easy to explore on foot. We then drove to Tarifa and spent the night.

The next morning, we took a fast ferry to Tangier, Morocco. After a day visit in Tangier, we spent the following day exploring Seville which is the fourth largest city in Spain. Seville contains several historical landmarks and was definitely a worthwhile visit. We had to wait a couple of days before we managed to board a return flight due primarily to C-5 airplane mechanical issues. I also discovered that I was able to use the hospital on base for a minor medical issue without any problem. On this trip, we learned that obtaining a rental car really expanded our opportunities for local exploration and it was a very simple process. During all of our Space-A trips, I was always able to use my U.S. driver's license to rent vehicles, although it is recommended that procuring an international driver's permit might help avoid possible issues. In the U.S., international driver permits are only legally issued by the American Automobile Association and the American Automobile Touring Alliance.

Germany

Our next family Space-A trip in 2010 finally landed us back in Germany. Rather than landing in the primary location of Ramstein, we landed in Spangdahlem which is about a 1.5-hour drive northwest of Ramstein. Given our previous experience with obtaining a rental car, we rented another car and were able to visit several cities in Germany including Oberammergau, Neuschwanstein, Garmisch-Partenkirchen, Heidelberg, and Stuttgart. Unfortunately, we were unable to get a room at the Edelweiss Lodge and Resort in Garmisch, but the lodge provided us with a list of other hotels and we had an enjoyable stay at another local hotel. We did manage to stay in military lodging in Stuttgart. When we obtained our rental car in Spangdahlem we ensured we would be allowed to return it at Ramstein. This action allowed for increased flexibility as we determined that there were many more Space-A flights from Ramstein than Spangdahlem. We were also pleasantly surprised by the Kaiserslautern Military Community Center (KMCC) which was finished in 2009 and is a huge complex with an AAFES Exchange, Ramstein Inn, German bakery, food court, rental car agencies, and even a four-plex movie theater. Since roll call for our flight back was at 1 am, we just hung out at the KMCC facility until departing. Doing some basic research on where we planned to visit beforehand allowed us to locate military facilities along our route that could provide us with resources such as lodging, restaurants, and tourist information. Having a rental car really complemented our trip as it allowed us more flexibility since we were constantly on the move.

Spain and Italy

Later that same year in 2010 my daughter had a week off school and we decided to attempt another Space-A adventure. The start of our trip landed us back in Rota, Spain. But when we landed, we noticed that there was another Space-A flight going to Aviano, Italy the next day. We managed to get on the flight to the Aviano Air Base in northeast Italy the follow day and easily obtained a room in the Mountain View Lodge on base. The next day we took a local shuttle to the town of Aviano nearby and purchased a train ticket from the local tobacco shop in the town center. Then we walked to the train station where we were the only people waiting. We had to transfer stations and eventually made it to Venice and arrived at the main Venice train terminal just as it was snowing.

After exploring Venice for a day, we returned to Aviano and found out that my daughter was not allowed to use the dining facility. When we went back to the lodge to get a room, we were told that the lodge was booked and we could wait until 9 pm on standby. Luckily the VIP room was not needed and we were able to rest in style in the two-room suite. The next day we determined that our best chance of returning to the U.S. was through Ramstein, Germany so we caught a flight to Ramstein and then eventually back to the U.S. The lessons learned during this trip was to conduct some basic research for any areas you might visit to help make for a better trip. Also, if you do not make any lodging reservations, you should always have some backup plans.

California

We decided to try using Space-A for a CONUS trip during my daughter's high school spring break in 2011. Our idea was to visit California. We managed to get a Space-A flight from Dover Air Force Base to Travis Air Force Base near Fairfield, California, southeast of Sacramento. Even though the base on Travis has a rental car agency, we determined there was a cheaper option just outside the main gate. Using a rental car, we explored San Francisco, Santa Barbara, Los Angeles, and Monterey. We were able to obtain military lodging in two locations during our travels. One was the Fort MacArthur Inn in Los Angeles and the second was the IHG Army Hotel on the Presidio of Monterey. We had no issues getting a return flight back to Dover.

California

Our previous trip to California was such a success that we decided to bring the entire family during the summer of 2011. Again, we traveled from Dover Air Force Base to Travis Air Force Base. This time around we obtained the rental car from the on-base agency and visited the local region to include San Francisco, Berkeley, and Sonoma. Our return flight was uneventful. Planning Space-A flights from major hubs or places that have a good quantity of flights increases the chances that your trip will prove less stressful and without the potential wasted days of waiting for flights.

Washington State

In 2012, I decided to visit my hometown in Washington State with my daughter during her spring break. We also planned to visit the town of Forks in Washington as Forks was the location for the popular Twilight book series that was popular at the time. When reviewing Space-A flights I noticed that there was a flight leaving Andrews Air Force Base only an hour from our house and going to Joint Base Lewis McChord (JBLM) in Washington State. We were surprised that when we were confirmed for roll call, we were told to board a small Beechcraft C-12 Huron plane. What was more surprising was that we would be traveling with a three-star general who was also on the plane along with his staff. The plane landed in a small regional airport for refueling and then finally landed at JBLM.

After getting a rental car and traveling around Washington State, we made our way back to McChord Field and managed to book lodging within walking distance of the passenger terminal. Eventually, we made it back to the East Coast but rather than returning to Andrews Air Force Base we landed in Dover Air Force Base in Dover, Delaware. It was quite the adventure getting back to our car parked at Andrews. First, we took a local bus that stopped outside the base gate of Dover Air Force Base to downtown Dover. Next, we took a regional bus to the train station in Wilmington, Delaware. Then we took a train to DC followed by a metro ride and finally a bus near the main gate of Andrews. We finished our trip by walking to the passenger terminal to retrieve our car. Again, flexibility is key when using Space-A travel.

Germany

As my daughter was getting ready to finish up college, her days as a dependent were ending and she would no longer be eligible for Space-A travel. In 2013, we took her final Space-A trip where we flew from Dover Air Force Base to Ramstein Germany and rented a car to visit cities in Germany like Baden-Baden. Luckily for us, my daughter was over 18. This came into play as when we attempted to book a room at Ramstein Inns, we were told that no rooms were being provided to families with children as several flight crews needed crew rest and children might interfere with the rest. What this little incident illustrates is that the rules are constantly changing and what might be true in the past might not be the current procedure.

Germany

The following year in 2014 I asked my son if he had any ideas for his spring break and whether he wanted to take a Space-A trip. He decided that he wanted to visit Switzerland, so we managed to get a Space-A flight from Dover to Ramstein, Germany and then obtained a rental car. We learned that if you drove a rental car into Switzerland you would need to purchase a Swiss motorway vignette. It is a sticker that you apply on the inside of the windshield of your car. We bought the vignette from a gas station right before the border and it cost about $40. We drove to Interlaken, Switzerland and found a great bread and breakfast place in town and had fun hiking in the mountains. On the way back to Ramstein, we took a detour and entered Basel, Switzerland. We parked our car in a parking garage in the town center (Stadt Mitte) and started exploring. We discovered that we were in Basel during the Carnival of Basel (Basler Fasnacht) which is the biggest carnival in Switzerland. What we discovered on that trip was that it can be worthwhile to explore as you may be pleasantly surprised.

Germany

Our most recent Space-A adventure occurred during my terminal leave when I was retiring from the military. My wife and I drove to Dover Air Force Base and began our journey by landing in Ramstein Air Force Base, Germany. In Ramstein Air Force Base, we took a taxi to the nearby town of Ramstein and then caught a train to Frankfurt. From Frankfurt, we took regional buses and trains throughout Europe to include Poland, Czech Republic, Hungary, Austria, Slovenia, Croatia, Italy, France, and Spain. In Italy, we were able to stay at the Ederle Inn in Vicenza, an Army lodging facility on Caserma Ederle, but otherwise used online hotel reservation programs to find hotels. In Spain, we returned to our old stomping grounds, Rota, and caught a flight that was going to San Diego, California. When we landed in San Diego we asked about possible future flights and were told that there was nothing scheduled for the next three days and there are not many flights leaving in the near future. We ended up getting a one-way rental car and driving to Travis Air Force Base and eventually getting a flight back to Dover Air Force Base and collecting our very dirty car in long-term parking.

What you may see illustrated in our Space-A journeys is that we learned something from each trip. With each additional Space-A experience we became more comfortable with the process and gained a greater understanding of the need for flexibility. We learned that there are no guarantees and that it is worthwhile to have a backup plan for your return trip and how you plan to endure until you eventually get a flight. The trips listed above show that we ultimately got to our destination and returned. On two occasions our Space-A trip plans gave way to our back-up plan. Once we attempted to fly to Germany from Dover but we either were not called or flights were canceled. After spending two days in the Dover area, visiting beaches and even the Delaware State Fair, we decided to cut our losses and vacation stateside. We visited Vermont and Montreal, Canada with no Space-A involved travel. On another occasion, we were attempting to fly on a Patriot Express flight out of BWI airport. There were a large number of people trying to get on the flight and it was very loud and packed. Unfortunately, we never heard our name called during roll call and when we went to the counter to investigate, we were told that it was too late and we would not be getting on the flight. Not every Space-A journey is successful but if you have patience, flexibility and some knowledge, it can be a marvelous adventure when it all comes together.

Space-A Trip Reports

If you read the chapter on our personal Space-A trips you gained a general understanding of what is possible utilizing Space-A travel. But our trips were limited to CONUS, Hawaii, Puerto Rico and certain parts of Europe. In order to truly grasp the far reach of Space-A travel, below are some examples of Space-A trips garnered from various Space-A trip reports. Space-A trip reports are when Space-A travelers document their Space-A adventures. You can read Space-A reports on various travel websites or look at the "Trip Reports Archives" and "Space-A Adventure US Trip Reports" Facebook groups. Reading about other adventures, especially if they are recent, will give you some great ideas for a future Space-A journey. If you already decided on a particular country, recent trip reports that went to the same country will provide you with information concerning current conditions on the ground. You may learn about the best local restaurants, tours, venues, transportation options, or restrictions.

Ireland

Shannon or Shannon Town is a town in County Clare, Ireland that contains the international Shannon Airport. Some Space-A flights do stop in Shannon en route to or from Europe but generally, passengers will either not be able to deplane or are restricted to a secure part of the terminal until the plane resumes its flight. For those rare cases where there is a flight that is manifested to Shannon, there are no typical military facilities that are available at most other locations and Shannon airport is a commercial airport.

Most Space-A travelers attempting to get to Ireland will first get to Ramstein, Germany and/or Mildenhall, England. From Mildenhall, you can either catch a commercial flight from London Heathrow

Airport to Dublin or rent a car and drive to the English west coast and then catch a ferry to Ireland.

One family with four children was able to catch a Space-A flight from Joint Base McGuire-Dix-Lakehurst, New Jersey to Shannon, Ireland. In Ireland, the family was able to rent a van for 60 Euros a day. They did not make any reservations before getting to Ireland and would simply find the first bread and breakfast establishment when they entered a town. Their lodging costs were between $100-120 per day and generally included a filling breakfast. They had great experiences staying at a B&B rather than a hotel. They finished their journey in Dublin where they returned their rental van and took a taxi to the Irish ferry. The family then took the three-hour Dublin to Holyhead ferry ride directly east. This ferry route is very popular and sells out at times so it is wise to get tickets as soon as possible. In Holyhead, Wales, the next leg of the journey was a train ride into London. Lodging in London will be expensive without prior reservations. After exploring London for a few days, the family of five managed to obtain a Ryan Air flight for only $300 for all of them going to Frankfurt, Germany. In Frankfurt, they rented another van to Ramstein and managed to obtain military lodging on base. They planned on flying to Dover, Delaware when a Space-A flight with 50 firm seats was announced. But ten seats were removed before boarding and the family was removed from the flight. They were confused why they were removed (bumped) as they were Category 3 and several Category 4 and 5 were not bumped. They found out later that they were incorrectly listed on the Space-A register as Category 5 rather than 3. This illustrates the importance of ensuring that you are correctly entered into the Space-A register. Fortunately, the family was able to get on a Space-A flight to McGuire the next day.

Italy

One retired couple with a Category 6 status, decided to visit Italy and attempted to fly from the U.S. east coast to Naples, Italy. Naval Support Activity Naples is a U.S. Navy military complex next to the Naples International Airport, about 2.5 hours south of Rome. The vacation plan was to visit the Amalfi Coast, Pompei and the town of Bari. As there were very few available Space-A flights during the time they planned to travel, they ended up getting a non-stop commercial flight from Boston to Rome for only $280 plus $25 for a checked bag.

Once in Italy, they got a rental car from Hertz through USAA for about $65 per day. They later realized that having a diesel vehicle rather than a gas-powered vehicle would have been more economical. Another important consideration when driving a car in Italy is parking. Parking within white lines is free and parking within yellow lines is restricted to residents. Blue lines indicate that you need to pay which is normally done with a ticket box where you then display the ticket on the vehicle dashboard.

After about two weeks, they returned their rental car at a location near a train station. They rented a B&B nearby and took a train the next day to another location. They had to change trains twice and had one train canceled. These types of train issues are common in Italy. When we were in Italy, we learned that after buying a paper train ticket at the train station for an unreserved regional train, you need to validate the ticket once you get on the train or you can get fined. Validating a paper ticket means simply inserting the ticket, arrow-end first, into a validating machine near the train entrance.

When it was time to leave Italy, the couple took an airport bus from Sorrento to Naples which dropped them off at the Naples airport. Then they got a taxi from Muto Travel, 39-339-161-8395, which is the only taxi service allowed on base. They managed to get on a Patriot Express flight that first went to Rota, Spain and then to Norfolk, Virginia. In Norfolk they took a local taxi, Coastal taxi, (757) 855-4-444, to stay at the Navy Lodge on Hampton Blvd and took another taxi the next day to Norfolk International Airport where they found a commercial flight back to their home.

This trip report contains several good lessons. First, it is important to be flexible and even if you cannot take Space-A round-trip to your desired destination, you may be able to use it for one leg of your journey. Second, the trip report provided some useful information about how to obtain a rental car, what type of model is preferable and local parking guidelines. Lastly, some bases have restrictions on which taxis are allowed to drive on base and having their phone number available can help expedite the process.

Greece and Spain

The location for Space-A travel in Greece is Naval Support Activity Souda Bay in Crete, Greece. It is the largest naval base for the U.S. and NATO in the eastern Mediterranean Sea. NSA Souda has a special base exit and entry procedure where you need to obtain an access number. After hours, this number is obtained from a security representative after the local security brief in the terminal. This number has an expiration date so when you get the number verify the expiration date. The Souda Bay passenger agents may or may not tell you about the requirement for an access number so obtain the security brief and access number before you leave the terminal.

A couple was attempting a Space-A adventure beginning from their home location in the southwestern U.S. This required them to first travel by commercial air and a variety of other local transportation options to get to Joint Base Andrews in Maryland. Since Uber is not allowed on Andrews, they hitchhiked from the main gate and spent a night at the Presidential Inn which is on-base lodging. The following day they obtained a one-way rental car from Enterprise which they drove to Norfolk, Virginia. They chose Enterprise as Enterprise has a counter in the passenger terminal on Andrews and will pick you up from the Presidential Inn to get your rental car. In Norfolk, they stayed in the Navy Lodge. The next morning, they drove to the Norfolk terminal and turned in the rental car by parking in the Enterprise parking spot outside the terminal and dropping the key outside the terminal door in the key box.

They were able to get on the Patriot Express flight and were manifested through to Souda. The flight took about 15 hours including 12 hours of flying and about three hours on the ground in Rota, Spain and Naples, Italy. They were able to obtain lodging at the Navy Lodge in Souda. They rented a car on base and were able to explore Crete for about two weeks staying primarily in lodging obtained via Airbnb.

The couple provided some additional information regarding base access. The base access code is a three-digit number that you give to the Greek security guards to get on base. The Code is only good for at most five days and unless you have a reason to be on the base you will not be given a code. Initially, they obtained a five-day code but when they went to renew the code, they were told they would only get a two-day code to check the flight schedule but could not come on the base if the only reason was to shop, eat, or use facilities like the laundry. You can also get an extended code if you are staying at on-base lodging. There is also a sign that says if your plane arrives after midnight you will not be allowed to leave the terminal until the next morning at 5 am when you can then be given the access code. Souda has a small shoppette, exchange, recreation facility, and a club with bar food options.

The couple was able to take a Patriot Express flight from Souda. The 90-minute flight to Naples was uneventful but then they spent three hours on the ground in Naples. The next scheduled leg was a 2.5-hour flight from Naples to Rota that ended up being a three-hour flight followed by five hours on the ground in Moron Air Base, Spain. The reason the plane was rerouted to Moron is that the Rota radar approach equipment failed. None of the passengers on the plane in Moron were able to disembark as the winds were too high for ground personnel to roll up the stairs to the plane. Eventually, the winds died down, the plane was refueled, and the plane flew to Rota. The couple then explored the local area to include Rota, Cadiz and Seville using a rental car obtained from the rental car agency located inside the Rota passenger terminal. At the end of their trip, they were able to fly on a C-17 that was going back to Norfolk and then caught a commercial flight back to their home.

During the couple's time in Spain, the wife got sick but was able to be treated in the Navy Hospital on Rota in the Emergency room as it was urgent and on the weekend. They experienced great care at the hospital. Personally, I was able to use the same hospital on one occasion for a minor issue and had a similarly pleasant experience. The couple mentioned that Rota requires a renewal of the base access pass every 48 hours. You get a paper pass for you and your vehicle that is good for the day of the pass and the next day until 2400 hours. Also, Space A visitors are only allowed to shop in the base shoppette which is fairly well stocked and can eat at the base pizza restaurant and club.

Singapore to Yokota to SeaTac

Based on information from trip reports, a possible adventure is traveling from Singapore to Yokota, Japan, and returning to the U.S. west coast. Singapore has a military airbase for the Republic of Singapore Air Force (RSAF) called Paya Lebar Air Base. The airbase was originally built in 1954 as the Singapore International Airport but was later transferred to the RSAF when the civilian airport moved to Changi.

Since Paya Lebar is a Singapore Air Base, Space-A passengers are only allowed to visit two buildings on base which are the AMC passenger terminal and the snack shop. Public transportation to the airbase consists of taking the Singapore Mass Rapid Transportation (MRT) to the Eunos Int station. Then take the SBS Transit Bus Service 94 from Sims Ave (Eunos Stn/Int) 12 stops to the Airport Road (Bef

Rsaf Roundabout) and walk the remaining distance to the gate. The airbase does not have any lodging facilities so Space-A travelers will need to obtain off base lodging or military lodging at PSA Sembawang which is approximately 45 minutes from the base. The base does have consistent Space-A flights to and from Yokota, Japan which is about one-hour west of Tokyo. The flights are both military and commercial chartered flights. Maintenance and weather issues as well as both U.S. and Singapore holidays can affect the flight schedules.

The couple attempting to travel using Space-A initially contacted the AMC representative at Paya Lebar and were informed that the flights were delayed due to a recent major storm. After spending two days in Singapore visiting local attractions, they arrived at the passenger terminal using a taxi and were pleasantly surprised when the seat count moved from 15 to 25 and then 40. They were not initially concerned as when they arrived at the passenger terminal there was only one other waiting couple. But as the time got closer to roll call, quite a few additional people appeared and the chances for a Category VI retiree seemed slim. But eventually they boarded a C-17 aircraft and flew the seven-hour flight to Yokota.

Yokota Air Base is a U.S. Air Force and Japan Air Self-Defense Force base in the city of Fussa, in western Tokyo. Lodging on base includes Kanto Lodge. Another option is Tokyo Recreational Lodging (Hardy Barracks) which is situated in a small U.S. Army Installation called Akasaka Press Center in the heart of Roppongi, Tokyo.

There is a process for going through Japanese immigration at Yokota. The Japanese immigration office at Yokota is located a short walk from the terminal. When you receive a stamp, it is only good for the calendar date of the stamp. If you are planning to get a Space-A roll call for a flight leaving early in the morning the next day, you may go to immigration the day prior and get your passport stamped with the date of the roll call. It is best to speak with the passenger terminal agents to ensure you have all the necessary documentation and follow the rules for that location. You may not be allowed to leave the terminal after selection for a flight.

If the flight situation from Yokota to the U.S. is challenging, consider flying to Osan, Korea to catch the Space-A flight scheduled for Travis Air Force Base, California. If you are in the lowest category, Category VI, retired military, you might have better luck getting on a flight from Korea, en route to Yokota and then to Travis AFB, rather than competing for the flight in Yokota as there could be less available seats after all the passengers board in Korea. The next available flight was a Patriot Express flight from Osan through Yokota to Seattle, Washington State with 41 firm seats that filled up quickly. Fortunately, the couple was able to get on the Patriot Express in Yokota rather than having to first fly to Osan.

In the trip report, the couple mentioned that they used the Virtual Roll Call (VRC) process for passenger selection. First, they marked themselves present at the passenger terminal counter and confirmed that their email address was correct. Then they waited for an emailed selection or non-selection notification to arrive. They received a selection email. The email contained all the information needed to check-in and receive a boarding pass. For that particular terminal, using VRC meant that passengers had to turn in their baggage the day before the flight. This means that passengers need to ensure they have any necessary clothes and toiletries in their carry-on bags to use until the following day. The next day the passengers simply walked into the terminal and waited to board the aircraft.

Micronesia

Micronesia is a subregion of Oceania which is composed of thousands of small islands in the western Pacific Ocean. You may recognize some of the islands such as the Mariana Islands, Marshall Islands, Palau, or Wake Island. The goal of one couple was to use Space-A travel to visit Micronesia.

First, the couple used commercial transportation to fly from the U.S. east coast to Sacramento, California. Then they took a shuttle from the Sacramento International Airport to Travis Air Force Base. They used Aloha Shuttle as it allowed them to be driven on base. After being dropped off at the Westwind Inn on base, the shuttle driver informed the couple that he would be glad to pick them up in the morning for the short drive to the passenger terminal which is less than a mile from the Inn.

Being a Category VI passenger, the couple made sure to sign up for Space-A travel 45 days before they began their journey. Everything appeared to go well after they were selected for a flight to Hawaii that had over 70 firm seats. They boarded the bus that then drove out to the aircraft. But then the bus suddenly returned back to the terminal. Due to earlier flight delays, the flight crew exceeded their flight duty period limits and the flight was rescheduled for the following day.

Fortunately, the couple kept tabs on the flight and soon learned that the planned afternoon flight was suddenly changed to an earlier morning flight. This demonstrates the need to keep current on flight schedules whenever you leave the passenger terminal as flight schedules can change quickly. They were able to fly in the passenger section of a C-5 Galaxy where the seats face backward toward the rear of the plane. They also noticed that the temperature in the front of the passenger section was quite cold whereas the back section near the lavatory was warm. We experienced this same temperature issue on our flight in a C-5. The flight to Hawaii from Travis took about five hours.

Now in Hawaii, the next focus was to get to Anderson Air Force Base, Guam. There was a recent aircraft accident in Guam so all flights into Guam were tentative. There was also no lodging available on Hickam Air Force Base so the couple decided to spend their time at the USO lounge at the Honolulu airport. Normally the Hickam passenger terminal closes at 10 pm unless there are late evening or early morning scheduled flights. They used Charlie's Taxi to get to the airport as it is one of the few taxi services that have access to the base. Another option to the commercial airport is to use a bus.

The USO at Honolulu airport has a sleeping room, a bank of computers with Wi-Fi access, a children's playroom, a shower, comfortable chairs, a big-screen TV and an abundance of snacks. They also offer a luggage storage area. The facility is open until midnight. Once the USO closed, the couple went upstairs to an area that the airport authority set aside for passengers with early morning flights, including passengers from Hickam. Once you sign in with your flight information (roll call times for Space-A passengers), you were free to find a vacant seat within the cordoned-off area.

The next morning the couple was able to get manifested to Guam. The flight included stops at Yokota Air Base, Japan and Kadena Air Base in Okinawa, Japan. They decided to purchase the box lunch for $5.50 that included the standard sandwich, fruit, apple sauce, juice, candy, chips, and bottled water. The stop at Yokota Air Base was brief but the stop at Kadena Air Base required an overnight stay. They decided to stay at the Shogun Inn on base and utilized the on-base taxi service to get around.

The couple finally reached their destination of Guam and made sure to note that the change in time zones meant that time in Guam was four hours earlier than in Hawaii and nine hours earlier than eastern standard time (EST). Even though Guam is a U.S. territory, they were still required to complete an entry form. They managed to get a ride with a fellow passenger from their flight to the Days Inn Guam which took about 40 minutes in traffic from the base. The couple took a taxi to get a rental car from the Guam International Airport and were able to explore the island. They also spent a few days at the Gateway Inn & Suites on Joint Region Marianas Naval Base Guam.

After enjoying Guam, the couple attempted to use Space-A to return back to the U.S. Their first potential flight was an aircraft with over 50 firm seats that was returning to the U.S. through Hawaii. But eventually, only a few seats ended up being released. Understanding that Space-A flights are tentative, the couple held on to their rental car keys and were able to extend the rental contract. That evening they stayed at the Royal Orchid Guam Hotel that also contains a USO Tumon Bay facility on the ground floor.

The next day the couple were able to board a Space-A flight heading to Hawaii. Since they expected to have a 23-hour stopover in Hawaii, they made reservations at the Navy Lodge on Ford Island in Hawaii shortly before takeoff. This is a tip that seasoned Space-A travelers use. Once you are fairly certain that you will be getting on a Space-A flight, make lodging reservations on the military base for the flight's destination. It was fortunate that they made these reservations because once the plane landed in Hickam, there were no available hotel reservations on base. They used Charlie's Taxi service once again for the short six-mile drive to the hotel and flew back to Travis AFB the next day.

Once the couple returned to Travis AFB, they decided to look for Space-A flights back to the east coast rather than automatically returning via commercial air out of Sacramento. They got lucky as there was a C-17 departing for Joint Base Charleston in South Carolina. Most of the Space-A passengers used the onboard sidewall troop seats but as there was plenty of space in the center of the plane, some passengers also were able to utilize the open space with air mattresses and blankets. Upon landing in Joint Base Charleston, the couple then managed to get a flight the next morning to Joint Base Andrews in Maryland.

Sicily and Greece

A retired couple decided to attempt to visit Sicily, Italy, the largest island in the Mediterranean Sea, using Space-A travel. They managed to board a C-40 out of Naval Air Station (NAS) Fort Worth Joint

Reserve Base, Texas that traveled with 57 passengers. They experienced a one-hour layover at St Johns, Newfoundland, Canada and then continued onward to Naval Air Station Sigonella in Sicily. The flight took about 12 hours in total.

When the couple attempted to call the Gateway Inn main toll-free number before the trip to make lodging reservations, they were told that there were no rooms available. But when they called the front desk directly, they managed to book five nights for only $60 per night. The Gateway Inn is located at NAS-I but the passenger terminal is located on NAS-2. The two different military areas are about ten miles apart. They were able to use the local dining facility called "The Galley" and met a 93-year-old WWII veteran that was traveling alone using Space-A.

The couple's travel recommendations are to carry an iPad for general use, install Skype for calling back to the U.S., using Dropbox to store important travel documents, bring a Garmin GPS unit w/ European data, and have a light backpack for daily traveling. They rented a car at the passenger terminal from Europcar. Their debit cards would not work at the two ATMs in NAS-2 so they joined the Navy Federal Credit Union in order to write a check and get cash. Then they had to drive to the Bank of America Community Bank to get Euros but were told that retirees were not eligible to buy Euros. He was actually breath tested for alcohol on the way out of NAS-1.

They were able to visit the nearby town of Catania and came away from the experience with mixed emotions. There was an abundance of trash everywhere and many non-functioning traffic lights. The basic idea when driving in an intersection is that whoever enters first has the right of way. Apparently, the drivers are very aggressive and most do not follow traffic laws, especially motorcycle drivers. Parking is difficult to find but if you find parking be sure to obtain a parking ticket and place the ticket in the vehicle window. There may be a government shuttle that goes to Catania. The next few days they visited Messina, Taormina,

Palermo, Greek-Roman ruins, the Duomo Cathedral "Monreale," and the Capella Palatine.

The couple read that Catania is the petty theft capital of Sicily and fellow Space-A travelers confirmed this when they recounted how they were subjected to a "bump and grab" theft while sitting in their car in traffic. When they were at a stop sign or light, a motorcyclist stopped in front of their car preventing their forward movement. When this happened, another motorcyclist opened the unlocked passenger door and retrieved a purse, iPhone, $100 in cash, credit cards, etc. from between the passenger's legs on the floor. The couple was unable to figure out how to lock their rental car doors. It is worthwhile to determine how to lock the car doors in a rental car before leaving the rental car agency.

While they were touring around Sicily, they kept tabs on Facebook about any regional flights going out of Sigonella NAS. They discovered that there were three flights scheduled for Souda Bay, Greece so they returned back to Sigonella. That is when they discovered that most gas stations are closed on Sundays. The first flight ended up being canceled. The second flight would not allow any Space-A passengers due to cargo restrictions. Then the third flight was also canceled. The passenger terminal agent asked if they wanted to fly on a 14 seat C-26 turboprop plane to Naples as there was a Patriot Express flight with plenty of seats scheduled from Naples to Souda Bay the following day. They managed to get on the flight to Naples and stayed at the Naples Gateway Inn.

The next day the Patriot Express flight had a tentative 60 seats to Naval Support Activity Souda Bay in Crete, Greece. The plane arrived late but eventually the couple boarded the plane in driving rain. When they called the Gateway Inn in Souda Bay from Naples, they were told there were no rooms. The passenger terminal agent in Souda Bay informed them it would be about a $40 taxi ride to downtown Chania and then another taxi ride back to base the next morning. Fortunately, they checked with the Gateway Inn and were told that they could get a Distinguished Visitor (DV) room. The Gateway Inn in Souda Bay allows Space-A reservations 30 days before arrival for a maximum of seven days and is a short walk from the passenger terminal. They had a rate increase in October 2018 that increased rates from $11-31 per night depending on the room type. The couple paid $80 for the DV room but the current rate for a deluxe queen on the Gateway Inn website shows $125.

The base on Souda Bay allows retirees to eat in the Fleet's Inn dining facility and the Spa Tours near the Navy Exchange has information on car rentals and tours. When renting a car from Spa Tours they do not allow you to forego the rental car loss damage waiver (CDW) and include full insurance coverage with their rates. You can also relax at the Liberty Arena which is a morale and welfare club with a small theater. When the couple moved from the DV room to a standard room to save on the cost, they discovered that the rooms were identical. They also learned the hard way that there is a Greek and U.S. side of the base and you need to have a four-digit security code to get on base. The couple also had challenges using GPS on the island. They noticed that the high season ends in August.

While in Crete the couple saw all the major sites to include visiting Heraklion which included the Palace at Knossos and an Archeological Museum. In Rethymno, they visited the Fortress (Fortesso). They had an enjoyable stay in the Sissy Village Resort. They highly recommend the Balos Beach Hotel in Kissamos. They took a seven-hour cruise by Balos Cruises from the Kissamos Port that went north up the peninsula and included a two hour stay at Gramvousa Island. They also visited the Crete Maritime Museum near the lighthouse in Chania and one of the best monasteries on the island about seven miles from the base that was built in 1820. They discovered that "Coffee Right" appeared to be the Starbucks of Greece.

When monitoring the passenger terminal Facebook site, they noticed that the next flights out were two flights to Ramstein,

Germany in two days' time. They planned to fly to Ramstein but then discovered that Ramstein did not have any available rooms and no future flights to Aviano AFB, Italy which was their next desired location. So, they extended their stay in Crete. But later they saw that the Ramstein flight was canceled. One service member informed them that the current situation in the Middle East was changing flight patterns which would affect Space-A flights.

Eventually, they were able to depart Souda Bay on a C-17 on a three-hour flight to Ramstein. They saw that there was another flight to Royal Air Force Mildenhall, England but made the decision to take the Germany flight instead. When flying Space-A, you will be constantly faced with decisions on which flights to take based on a variety of factors such as likelihood of the flight departing, being able to get on the plane, destination and lodging availability, and other reasons. They were able to leave their rental car at the passenger terminal and discovered that the terminal had free Wi-Fi. They were unable to speak with a lodging representative at Ramstein.

When the couple arrived in Ramstein there was a one-hour wait for all the people that were attempting to get a room at Ramstein Lodging. They noticed that there was a difference between attempting to make reservations in person and by phone. One person in line informed them that due to some military locations in Germany being closed down there is a greater need for temporary lodging at Ramstein. There will always be a variety of factors that affect availability such as high season versus low season or global considerations. One American they spoke with that was living in Germany for the past 35 years, told them that a new hospital was planned which would ensure the operation of Ramstein for many years to come. Based on an article in the Stars and Stripes in 2014, a new, nearly billion-dollar U.S. military hospital is being built to replace the aging Landstuhl Regional Medical Center and the Air Force's medical clinic at Ramstein Air Base with a planned completion date of 2022. They also learned about a shuttle that runs all around Ramstein Village is generally available every 20 minutes.

This trip report demonstrates the importance of doing a little research on your planned Space-A destination to ensure you have a more enjoyable experience. Each base will have its own particular requirements and limitations. Reading trip reports and reports from Space-A websites will help with a smoother journey and give you options to consider.

Korea

The goal for this couple was to reach Korea from the east coast of the U.S. The first leg of their journey was to take a commercial flight from North Carolina to Seattle, Washington. They planned to take a Patriot Express flight that was scheduled to leave SeaTac International Airport in Seattle to Osan Air Base, a U.S. Air Force Base in Pyeongtaek, South Korea about 40 miles south of Seoul. They spent two nights at a friend's house and then due to an early morning roll call, spent the next day camped out at the SeaTac USO. The SeaTac USO is the busiest USO airport center in the U.S. and is open 24 hours due to the support of over 200 volunteers.

The couple managed to get manifested on their intended flight and reached Osan in the afternoon. Then they took a taxi to Songtan station where they boarded a 3.5-hour train to the town of Daegu and Camp Walker in order to visit a relative stationed in Korea. The nearest subway station for Camp Walker is Hyeonchungno, located on the northwest side of the base outside Gate 6. Camp Walker is a collection of U.S. military bases in Daegu that also include Camp Henry and Camp George. They were able to obtain lodging at the Camp Walker Army Lodge and explore the local area.

After completing their visit in Daegu, they took a three-hour train ride to Seoul, the capital of South Korea. They were able to spend several days at the Dragon Hill Lodge. The Dragon Hill Lodge is a

DoD owned hotel in Seoul, South Korea. It is part of the Yongsan Garrison military community. The lodge is an Armed Forces Recreation Center (AFRC) resort hotel. If you are planning on staying at the Dragon Hill Lodge, it is worthwhile to check their special offers website page as they have several lodging and tour programs and other specials. The couple discovered that the Yongsan Garrison was fairly empty during their visit. They purchased the five-night and six-day package from Dragon Hill Lodge which consists of four free tours. They chose the Seoul Tower, Demilitarized Zone (DMZ), Korean Folk Village and downtown temple tours.

They were unsuccessful in leaving Korea on another Patriot Express flight so they continued to explore South Korea including a visit to Namdaemun Market which is the largest traditional market in Korea. They took a train to the town of Busan to see a huge sand sculpture festival on the beach. They tried again for another Patriot Express flight but missed manifest by only five people. They then executed their plan B which was to purchase commercial tickets back to Seattle and then back to the east coast. They found it extremely easy to navigate the trains and subways in South Korea. The subway and train stations are announced in both Hangul and English. Korea uses a rechargeable card for all travel in Korea (including taxis' in Seoul), you can easily recharge your travel card at any station, but you have to use cash.

Other

Some adventurous Space-A travelers might be able to fly all the way down under to Australia. The general route begins at Travis Air Force Base in California or another location that has a Space-A flight going to Hickam Air Force Base, Honolulu, Hawaii. Then from Hickam AFB, you can attempt for a direct flight to Royal Australian Air Force (RAAF) Richmond, Australia or through Anderson Air Force Base, Guam.

Some old-timers have stories about using Space-A to fly into Christchurch, New Zealand. The primary issue with flying to or from Christchurch was that if the plane landed in Australia for a remain overnight (RON) or refueling, all the passengers were required to have an Australian visa. Without the visa, the passengers were not allowed on the flight.

Other Space-A travelers reminisce about taking flights down to South America. Most of the flights to South America were called Embassy Runs and have been generally discontinued although the very rare, occasional flight might get scheduled. One current possibility is to get close to South America by attempting to fly into Honduras in Central America. Soto Cano Air Base also known as Palmerola Air Base is a Honduran military base about five miles south of Comayagua in Honduras. The base contains the U.S. military's Joint Task Force Bravo (JTF-B). Space-A flights to Honduras originate from Joint Base Charleston, South Carolina.

General Travel Tips

Below are some travel tips that you may want to consider when traveling to help make your experience more enjoyable.

Cell Phones

Most U.S. cell phone carriers have an international plan that you can activate while overseas. The costs will vary depending on your cell phone provider, where you are traveling and how you plan to use your cell phone. Some plans even have free data and texting while overseas. It is best to check with your carrier for the particulars.

Another option is to purchase a pre-paid cell phone in the country you are visiting. This may make sense if you plan to either stay in one country for an extended period or will only be traveling to countries that make use of that cell phone. You will readily find inexpensive prepaid cell phones at overseas kiosks with different costs and features.

A third choice is to replace the Subscriber Identify Module (SIM) card in your existing phone. A SIM card is a small card containing a chip that allows your cell phone to tap into a specific mobile network. You can remove the SIM card from your U.S. wireless service carrier by inserting a pin or paper clip into the small hole on the side of your phone and replacing it with an international SIM card. When you take out your U.S. SIM card, you will get a new number from the country where you purchased the card, and you will be unable to call or text with your U.S. number. But you will usually pay significantly less for cellular data using a local SIM card. You will also need to either have an unlocked cell phone or request that your carrier unlock your currently locked phone before you travel.

There are two different networks, the Global System for Mobile Communications (GSM) and the Code Division Multiple Access (CDMA). Cell phone carriers in the U.S. use both networks. The network in Europe is only GSM so if you have a cell phone with CDMA it will not work in Europe. If you are unsure whether your cell phone will work overseas, contact your carrier.

The final option is to rely only on Wi-Fi. This is the option that we use as we are constantly on the move between countries. We simply place our cell phones on airplane mode. Depending on your travel destination, you will generally be able to find decent Wi-Fi service. Starbucks and McDonalds are two reliable overseas locations with free Wi-Fi service. We then used several different Wi-Fi based apps for communications. Our carrier would also allow us to send free text messages while overseas and my GPS also worked even while in airplane mode.

Credit and Debit Cards

When deciding on a credit card my suggestion is to get either a Mastercard or Visa credit card as they are accepted worldwide wherever credit cards are accepted and are the two largest card networks in the world. If you will be traveling overseas you should also ensure that your credit card does not have foreign transactions fees. Foreign transaction fees, also called international transaction fees, are charged to cardholders when they purchase items while overseas or when they make purchases that use an overseas bank to process the transaction. Usually, foreign transaction fees are about 3%.

Although credit cards are accepted worldwide, there are some locations or businesses that only operate with cash. If you need to get cash overseas, you will generally get the best exchange rate by using your debit card at an ATM. If possible, attempt to obtain any necessary cash from the ATM or financial institution on base.

If your ATM card is linked to the PLUS, Cirrus or Maestro networks, you have the option of using it to obtain cash in hundreds of countries worldwide. The PLUS network is associated with Visa, so your Visa card will usually work at those ATMs. The Cirrus and

Maestro networks are associated with MasterCard, and so ATMs marked with these logos usually accept MasterCard for cash advances. The majority of ATMs accept cards from any of these major networks.

Sudden changes in your account activity, such as frequent withdrawals in a foreign country using your debit card, can sometimes trigger a fraud alert and cause your bank to freeze your account. To prevent being stranded overseas without a functioning debit card, call your bank before you leave to let them know where and when you will be traveling. You want to do the same thing for your credit card.

When deciding how much to withdraw, try to choose an uneven amount so you do not wind up with larger bills that are difficult to use. For example, withdraw 280 euros rather than 300 euros.

Virtual Private Network (VPN)

Most travelers are heavily reliant on public Wi-Fi when they travel but unfortunately public Wi-Fi is susceptible to hackers and malicious websites. Public Wi-Fi can be compromised almost anywhere, including on military bases, airports, restaurants and local businesses. If you want to protect your information and secure your privacy, you may want to consider a Virtual Private Network (VPN). A VPN allows you to create a secure connection to another network over the Internet. VPNs can be used to access region-restricted websites, shield your browsing activity from prying eyes on public Wi-Fi, and even stream popular media like Netflix and Hulu while overseas. If your VPN is "tunneled" to the United States, then you will be able to browse the internet as if you are in the United States even though you may be in another country. Some possible VPN services include:

- TunnelBear
- ExpressVPN
- CyberGhost
- NordVPN

- IPVanish
- PrivateVPN

Portable Power Bank

A power bank is a portable device where can supply power from its built-in battery through a USB port. Having a spare source of power is critical when traveling and using a variety of power-hungry devices like laptops, phones, cameras, and other devices. Having multiple USB ports on the power bank increases functionality. Power banks come in a variety of sizes and you will need to determine the proper tradeoff between weight and capacity. The power capacity is measured in milliamp hours or mAh and common capacity ratings range from 2,000 mAh to 20,000 mAh. For example, a Samsung Galaxy S8 can be charged approximately 4.5 times with a 20,000 mAh power bank.

Retractable USB Cables

More public places and even some hotels now offer the ability to charge your electronic devices using the universal serial bus (USB) which is a standard technology for attaching peripheral devices. But sometimes short cables will not reach or long cables are too cumbersome. You increase your flexibility when charging your electronic devices and avoid the need for multiple country-specific plugs by using retractable USB cables. By being retractable you avoid the constant tangles of regular cables.

Dual USB Car Charger

If you plan to use a vehicle on your travels, you may also consider bringing a USB car charger that installs in the vehicle's cigarette lighter port. They are available with multiple USB ports and some will even charge 2-3 times faster than the standard vehicle USB connections.

This is definitely a necessity if you are using your cell phone for navigation while driving in order to avoid draining your cell phone battery.

Smartphone Car Mount

If you plan to use a rental car while traveling you may consider bringing a cell phone car cradle. This device will hold your cell phone in position while driving so you can easily follow navigation directions. The simplest version consists of the type that clips into a vehicle vent on the dashboard. The mount can wrap around the cell phone or some versions are magnetic. The magnetic versions are very easy to use and normally come with a thin magnet that attaches between your cell phone and the cell phone case.

Travel Applications (Apps)

Almost everybody has a cell phone nowadays and take them when traveling. There are several mobile applications or apps that help make traveling a much better experience. From trip planners to online marketplaces for flights and hotels, there are several available travel apps designed to help make your adventures truly remarkable and worry-free.

GPSmyCity

This handy app presents you with over 6,500 self-guided walks in over 1,000 cities around the world, featuring the best of each city, from world-famous attractions to hidden gems. This is a great way to see a city on foot, at your own pace and at a fraction of the cost you would normally pay for a guided tour. The app serves the needs of travelers who enjoy exploring new cities on foot, whether alone or accompanied by a local guide. It features self-guided city walks and GPS-powered travel articles. The guided tours feature connects with knowledgeable local guides who can show you around to local attractions, markets, food, places of culture, and nightlife venues, as well as share local insider knowledge.

www.gpsmycity.com[1]

Facebook Messenger

Facebook Messenger (FM) allows for phone or video calls and the ability to share photos and videos. One good feature about FM is that you do not need a Facebook account as it is a separate app. You can establish an account using your cell phone number. FM is an easy way to connect with people you meet on your travels. You can create a

---

1.   http://www.gpsmycity.com

contact by just searching for a name without the need for a phone number and you do not need to be a friend on Facebook.

www.messenger.com

WhatsApp

WhatsApp Messenger is a free messaging app owned by Facebook. WhatsApp uses your phone's internet connection to send messages and make calls. A WhatsApp account is associated with your mobile telephone number and all communication is encrypted. Switch from Short Message Service (SMS) to WhatsApp to send and receive messages, calls, photos, videos, documents, and voice messages. WhatsApp calls use your phone's Internet connection rather than your cellular plan's voice minutes to make free calls although data charges may apply. There are no extra charges to send WhatsApp messages internationally.

Since WhatsApp is a telephony app, iPod and iPad are not supported devices. Also, you must establish your WhatsApp account while you are still connected to your mobile network. The service sends you a text with a code to verify your phone number. If you cannot receive the text, you cannot complete the account set-up process.

We did not use WhatsApp until our son was visiting Korea and it was the best way for us to communicate with him overseas. Once we activated our account, we noticed that several people we knew in Germany also contacted us with the app as it was their preferred means to communicate in Germany.

www.whatsapp.com

Skype

Skype is a telecommunications app owned by Microsoft that specializes in providing video chat and voice calls between computers, tablets, and mobile devices via the Internet. Skype also provides instant messaging services. Users may transmit text, video, audio, and images.

When you are overseas and need to contact a company back in the U.S. that has a toll-free number, you can use Skype to dial those toll-free numbers with Wi-Fi and the call will be free. Another travel hack is to use Skype to call the toll-free number from a U.S. based phone carrier prepaid calling card and then make a call to any phone number in the world at a much-reduced rate. Most prepaid calling cards also offer military discounts.

For a nominal cost, you can purchase a phone number from Skype which allows friends and family to call you just as if they were calling a regular cell phone number. But you have to be connected to Wi-Fi to use this feature.

Features:

- Use Skype to call phones - Call landlines and mobiles from anywhere in the world at low rates
- Skype Number - Get a local phone number in another country or region and answer calls
- HD video calling - One to one or group video calling.
- Live subtitles - Read the words that are spoken during an audio or video call
- Mobile screen sharing - Share anything from presentations to photos during a call
- Skype call recording - Capture Skype calls

www.skype.com/en

Line

Line is similar to WhatsApp and allows for messaging and free voice and video calls. It is the primary Wi-Fi calling service used in Japan and states it has a number one ranking in 52 countries. You must establish your account while still in the U.S.

Features:

- Group video calls
- Face to face video chats
- Create polls
- Free voice and video calls
- Share messages, photos, videos, stickers, voice messages, and locations
- Store messages, photos, videos, and more in Keep
- Place international calls to mobile phones and landlines at low rates

line.me/en

Google Maps

Google Maps is a web mapping service developed by Google. It offers street maps, 360° panoramic views of streets (Street View), real-time traffic conditions, and route planning for traveling by foot, car, bicycle or public transportation.

The route planning feature is not only helpful in real-time but can be used to plan future trips. We use it all the time to determine when we will need to leave to get to a particular location at a certain time and also what transportation option to utilize such as whether to grab an Uber, take the metro, or drive. In some parts of the world, you can use Google Maps offline by downloading a local version of the map. We used this feature before to help when driving through a known area that had limited GPS and it worked quite well.

Features:

- Directions and transit – Route planner

- Traffic conditions – Crowdsourced traffic information
- Street View – 360-degree panoramic street-level views of various locations
- 45° imagery – 45-degree aerial imagery offering a bird's eye view of certain cities
- Business listings – Collated business listings from multiple on-line and off-line sources
- Indoor maps – Aids in navigating within buildings such as airports, museums and other public spaces
- My Maps – Ability to create custom maps
- Google Local Guides – Allows users to contribute reviews, photos and basic information

www.google.com/maps[2]

Maps.me

Maps.me (formerly named MapsWithMe) is a free mobile app that provides offline maps using OpenStreetMap data. This is a great mapping app for when you will not have Wi-Fi access but still need the ability to navigate your surroundings. You do have to plan ahead by downloading all the maps and routing for the areas you plan to visit before you depart. There is no need for a Wi-Fi or network connection because it is GPS based.

Features:

- Offline map data that is updated approximately 1-2 times per month
- GPS support
- Offline search (by name, address, category, and coordinates)
- Offline routes for cars, foot, bicycle, and subway
- Map Editor (OpenStreetMap.org)

- Bookmarks (with cloud back up option)
- Auto-follow mode
- Location and bookmarks sharing
- Travel guides
- Car traffic

maps.me

Rome2rio

Rome2rio is an online transport search engine that launched in 2011. Rome2rio is a worldwide platform capable of long-distance (inter-city) trip planning as well as local (intra-city) journey planning. Users can input any address, town or landmark as the origin and destination and Rome2rio searches a database of flight, train, ferry, bus and driving routes to present route and price options for traveling to that destination.

The transport data searched by Rome2rio includes:

- Over 717,000 bus routes via about 3,300 bus operators
- Over 207,000 train lines via about 360 train operators
- Over 54,000 flight paths via about 650 airlines
- Over 12,000 ferries via about 530 ferry operators

It also provides estimated travel times and price ranges along with links to the providers' websites to confirm schedules and book reservations. Rome2rio has a web-based version and an app. You must be connected to the internet to use Rome2rio.

www.rome2rio.com[3]

---

3.   http://www.rome2rio.com

Google Translate

Google Translate is a free multilingual machine translation service developed by Google. It offers a website interface and mobile apps. Google Translate supports over 105 languages at various levels. The app is not perfect and will make occasional mistakes but I noticed that it definitely keeps improving its accuracy over time. The big improvements came in 2016 when Google used a neural machine translation engine.

Features:

- Written Words Translation - A function that translates written words or text to a foreign language
- Website Translation - A function that translates a whole webpage to selected languages
- Document Translation - A function that translates a document uploaded by the users to selected languages
- Speech Translation - A function that instantly translates spoken language into the selected foreign language
- Mobile App Translation – This feature called "Tap to Translate," made instant translation accessible inside any apps without exiting or switching it
- Image Translation - A function that identifies text in a picture taken by the users and translates text on the screen instantly by images
- Handwritten Translation - A function that translates language that is handwritten on the phone screen or drawn on a virtual keyboard without the support of a keyboard

translate.google.com

Airbnb

Airbnb is an online marketplace for offering lodging, tours, classes, workshops, tourism experiences or even restaurant reservations. The company does not own any of the real estate listings. It acts as a broker, receiving commissions from each booking. Airbnb is a shortened version of its original name, AirBedandBreakfast.com.

www.airbnb.com[4]

Booking.com

Booking.com is a travel fare aggregator website and travel metasearch engine for lodging reservations. You can use it to find hotel deals and book your accommodation easily online. The site has over 27 million listings in 228 countries and territories.

www.booking.com[5]

Hotels.com

Hotels.com is a website for booking hotel rooms online and by telephone. The company has 85 websites in 34 languages and lists over 325,000 hotels in approximately 19,000 locations. Its inventory includes hotels and B&Bs, and some condos and other types of commercial lodging. They use "Captain Obvious" as their advertising spokesman and have a loyalty program. Hotels.com is part of Expedia.

www.hotels.com[6]

Google Flights

Google Flights is an online flight booking search service that facilitates the purchase of airline tickets through third-party suppliers. An

---

4.   http://www.airbnb.com

5.   http://www.booking.com

6.   http://www.hotels.com

innovation of Google Flights is that it allows open-ended searches based on criteria other than the destination such as a range of dates. When selecting a destination, Google Flights will calculate every price for each day of the next 12 months using a graph or table. This allows users to easily spot the cheapest date to fly to their destination. Competitors include Expedia, Orbitz and Kayak.com.

Features:

- Discover new destinations with the explore map
- Email price alerts
- Ability to filter search - stops, duration, time, and interests
- Fly from a different airport
- Check your legroom

www.google.com/flights[7]

Hopper

The mobile-only app Hopper tracks flight prices and gives you periodic updates on whether you should buy now or wait. They state that they can predict prices with 95% accuracy up to one year in advance. It does not just tell you to wait to buy your ticket but gives you a date when the price will likely rise.

www.hopper.com[8]

HotelTonight

HotelTonight is an online travel app that allows users to find discounted hotel accommodations throughout the world. This travel app specializing in selling same-day hotel reservations. Due to the

---

7.   http://www.google.com/flights

8.   http://www.hopper.com

last-minute nature of the bookings, the app can offer deep discounts off the listed hotel rate. The company was acquired by Airbnb.

www.hoteltonight.com[9]

TripAdvisor

TripAdvisor is a travel and restaurant website company that shows hotel and restaurant reviews, accommodation bookings and other travel-related content. It also includes interactive travel forums. TripAdvisor is the largest "social travel website" in the world. It is a comprehensive online resource for travelers, with background information about different cities and regions, plus highlights of what to see and do. It has reviews written by members of the TripAdvisor community, as well as photos from their travels so you know what to expect before you arrive. It used to be a part of Expedia.

www.tripadvisor.com[10]

Uber

Uber, is a multinational ride-hailing company offering services that include peer-to-peer ridesharing, ride service hailing, food delivery, and even electric bikes and scooters. The company has operations in over 785 metropolitan areas worldwide and its platforms can be accessed via its websites and mobile apps. There are a few reasons that ride-on-demand apps work so well for travelers. First, it eliminates the need to carry local currency. Second, you do not have to speak the same language as your driver to get to where you need to go. Third, there is no haggling. Depending on the country you are visiting, you may want to research other riding hailing companies that operating in the area such as Grab (Philippines, Vietnam, Malaysia, Indonesia and Myanmar), DidiChuxing (China), and Ola (India).

---

9.   http://www.hoteltonight.com

10.   http://www.tripadvisor.com

<u>www.uber.com</u>[11]

Wikitravel

Although not an app, Wikitravel is a helpful guide for world travelers. It is a project designed to create a free and reliable world-wide travel guide. It is built in collaboration with travelers from around the globe.
<u>wikitravel.org/en</u>/

---

11.   http://www.uber.com

Lodging

Once you reach your travel destination, you will need to have a place to sleep. Fortunately, there are several choices available. If you qualify for Space-A travel, you will most likely also be eligible for military lodging. Each military service will have its own particular lodging services.

Air Force

The CONUS only toll-free number for Air Force Lodging Reservations is 888-AF-LODGE (888-235-6343). The Air Force offers more than 27,000 rooms at 89 locations worldwide. You can either call the phone number or consult the Air Force Lodging Directory which provides specific on-base lodging information for each Air Force facility around the world.

Army

There are almost 22,000 Army lodging units, temporary housing, and guesthouses at 80 locations in the United States, Korea, Japan, Belgium, Germany, Italy, Alaska, and Hawaii. You can make reservations through the Central Reservation Center: 800-GO-ARMY-1 (800-462-7691) (commercial: 256-313-2790). The Army MWR website contains lodging information for all Army facilities worldwide. The site also has information on the Lodging Success Program (LSP), which offers special rates for hotels located near Army installations. This program offers hotels in Atlanta, San Antonio, the National Capital Region, Hampton, Newport News, Miami and Puerto Rico.

Marine Corps

Reservations for the Marine Corps transient billeting quarters are accepted on an as-received basis for all authorized patrons. All others will be billeted on a Space-A basis. Reservations for Temporary Lodging Facilities are recommended as many Lodging Facilities are booked far in advance. Reservation policies vary among facilities. The Marine Corps lodging websites are the best way to obtain information about available lodging.

Navy

The Navy Lodging Program consists of 1) Navy Lodges, 2) Navy Gateways Inns & Suites, and 3) Navy Getaways. The Navy operates 40 Navy Lodges on bases worldwide. Navy Gateway Inns & Suites (NGIS) has over 22,000 guest rooms worldwide. The room rates and types vary based on location. At select locations NGIS has partnered with commercial hotels offering rates at or below per diem. Navy Getaways include vacation rentals, cabins, townhomes, condos, bunkhouses, and resort-style vacation as well as RV & tent sites.

The toll-free number for the Navy Lodge Central Reservation Center (CRC) is 1-800-NAVY-INN (628-9466). Located at the Jacksonville, Florida Naval Air Station, the CRC is available 24 hours a day, 7 days a week. They also produce the Navy Lodge Worldwide Directory.

Coast Guard

There is no central reservations office for Coast Guard facilities, but you can find contact information for each recreation area in the Coast Guard MWR Recreational Lodging Facilities Guide. When attempting to locate military lodging, I always start with the Army, Navy and Air Force and completely forget the Coast Guard. When visiting Key West recently we used Navy lodging facilities as the majority of military facilities in Key West are Navy related. But I was surprised to discover that the Coast Guard actually has four cottages and RV pads located at USCG Station Marathon which is close to Key West, Florida.

Armed Forces Recreation Centers

Armed Forces Recreation Centers (AFRC) provide resort-style facilities to members of the military. The locations include Dragon Hill Lodge in Korea, Edelweiss Lodge and Resort in Germany, Hale Koa Hotel in Hawaii and Shades of Green in Walt Disney World Resort in Florida. We stayed in three of these resorts and always experienced great resort-like experiences.

American Forces Travel

American Forces Travel is a joint service program that offers online travel reservations. The services contracted with Priceline to provide travel benefits to the U.S. military community. It is the only official joint services MWR leisure travel website.

Armed Forces Vacation Club

Armed Forces Vacation Club (AFVC) offers vacations to all eligible members of the U.S. military. They have rental options in destinations worldwide, including $349 weeklong Space-A stays. Free membership is available to members of the military.

Other

Another option to secure lodging is to use online reservation services such as Hotels.com, Booking.com or Airbnb that were mentioned in the Travel Applications chapter. On one of our Space-A adventures, we landed in Germany and made hotel reservations online either the day before or on the actual day that we needed a place to stay and never had an issue. This allowed us maximum flexibility as we traveled throughout Europe for about two months. A key to our success was only booking with hotels that contained good reviews.

Most AMC terminals will publish a current fact sheet called an "AMCGRAM." These fact sheets provide helpful information about that particular location including terminal hours, long-term parking instructions, contact numbers for local lodging, rental cars, and other amenities. The lodging information contained in the AMCGRAM is a good starting point for securing lodging. The reference section includes a website link for an example AMCGRAM.

Starting in October 2019, The DoD required certain lodging facilities to change their fiscal operating structure which meant that prices at certain facilities experienced significant increases. This change did not include every military lodging option. For instance, Navy Lodges and most Army Lodging run by IHG were not affected. This change just means that you have to be a savvy traveler and check all your lodging options and not assume that the military lodging choice will be the least costly or best value. But it can be difficult to compete with some of the benefits of military lodging that include: no taxes, free parking, generally secure and safe, and access to shoppettes or other facilities like gyms, laundry facilities, etc.

Some additional lodging tips are to keep alert for military lodging or hotel chain promotions. The best way to learn about these promotions is to register for all the major hotel chain loyalty programs. If you primarily book with one hotel chain, you may also accumulate points that can be used for free nights. Some hotel chains have their own credit card which also allows you to generate points which in turn can be used for free or reduced-cost rooms. It also does not hurt to ask if the hotel offers any military discounts. One particular feature that we look for in a hotel is free Wi-Fi and free breakfast. These two features can help you lower your overall expenses. If you plan to stay in one location for more than a few days, it may be worthwhile to look for short-term rentals of furnished apartments or houses. This is where using services like Airbnb, Armed Forces Vacation Club, or other locally available services could outweigh the daily costs of a hotel.

References

Directives and Instructions

Air Mobility Command Instruction 24-101 Volume 14
    static.epublishing.af.mil/production/1/amc/publication/amci24-101v14/amci24-101v14.pdf

Defense Transportation Regulation, Part V, Department of Defense Customs and Border Clearance Policies and Procedures
    www.ustranscom.mil/dtr/part-v/dtr_part_v_501.pdf[1]

Department of Defense Directive (DoDD) 1000.21: DoD Passport and Passport Agent Services
    www.hsdl.org/?abstract&did=467111[2]

Department of Defense Instruction (DODI) 1327.06 (Leave and Liberty Policy and Procedures)
    www.esd.whs.mil/Portals/54/Documents/DD/issuances/dodi/132706p.pdf[3]

Air Mobility Command Instruction 24-101, Volume 14, Military Airlift Passenger Service
    static.epublishing.af.mil/production/1/amc/publication/amci24-101v14/amci24-101v14.pdf

Department of Defense Directives Division - Various forms, manuals, directives, and instructions
    www.esd.whs.mil/dd/[4]

---

1.   http://www.ustranscom.mil/dtr/part-v/dtr_part_v_501.pdf

2.   http://www.hsdl.org/?abstract&did=467111

3.   http://www.esd.whs.mil/Portals/54/Documents/DD/issuances/dodi/132706p.pdf

4.   http://www.esd.whs.mil/dd/

Websites

AMC Passenger Terminal Phone Directory and Contact Information (See link on webpage)

www.amc.af.mil/Home/AMC-Travel-Site/[5]

Department of State – Passports

travel.state.gov/content/travel/en/passports.html/

Department of State – Visas and Country Information

travel.state.gov/content/travel/en/international-travel/ International-Travel-Country-Information-Pages.html

International Driving Permit

www.aaa.com/vacation/idpf.html[6]

Department of Defense Lodging

www.dodlodging.net/[7]

IHG Army Hotels

www.ihg.com/armyhotels/hotels/us/en/reservation[8]

U.S. Army Morale, Welfare and Recreation (MWR)

www.armymwr.com/[9]

USMC Temporary Lodging Facilities

www.usmc-mccs.org/services/lodging/temporary-lodging-facilities/[10]

Marine Corps Transient Housing

marines.dodlodging.net/

Navy Lodge

www.navy-lodge.com/[11]

Navy Gateway Inns & Suites

---

5.   http://www.amc.af.mil/Home/AMC-Travel-Site/

6.   http://www.aaa.com/vacation/idpf.html

7.   http://www.dodlodging.net/

8.   http://www.ihg.com/armyhotels/hotels/us/en/reservation

9.   http://www.armymwr.com/

10.   http://www.usmc-mccs.org/services/lodging/temporary-lodging-facilities/

11.   http://www.navy-lodge.com/

ngis.dodlodging.net/
Navy Getaways
get.dodlodging.net/
Coast Guard Lodging
www.dcms.uscg.mil/Our-Organization/Assistant-Commandant-for-Human-Resources-CG-1/Community-Services-Command-CSC/MWR/Coast-Guard-Lodging/[12]
American Forces Travel
www.americanforcestravel.com/[13]
Armed Forces Recreation Centers
www.armymwr.com/travel/armed-forces-hotels-resorts[14]
Defense Travel Management Office
www.defensetravel.dod.mil/site/govLodging.cfm[15]
AMC Pet Travel Information Page
www.amc.af.mil/Home/AMC-Travel-Site/AMC-Pet-Travel-Page/[16]
AAFES Exchange Overseas Privileges
www.aafes.com/exchange-stores/overseas[17]
Commissary FAQs
www.commissaries.com/customer-service/faqs[18]

Forms and Letters

AMC Space-A Email Sign-up Form

---

12.   http://www.dcms.uscg.mil/Our-Organization/Assistant-Commandant-for-Human-Resources-CG-1/Community-Services-Command-CSC/MWR/Coast-Guard-Lodging/

13.   http://www.americanforcestravel.com/

14.   http://www.armymwr.com/travel/armed-forces-hotels-resorts

15.   http://www.defensetravel.dod.mil/site/govLodging.cfm

16.   http://www.amc.af.mil/Home/AMC-Travel-Site/AMC-Pet-Travel-Page/

17.   http://www.aafes.com/exchange-stores/overseas

18.   http://www.commissaries.com/customer-service/faqs

<u>www.amc.af.mil/Home/AMC-Travel-Site/AMC-Space-Available-Travel-Page/</u>[19]
Unaccompanied Command Sponsor Letter
<u>www.amc.af.mil/Portals/12/documents/AFD-140922-057.pdf?ver=2016-05-18-115438-263</u>[20]
Non-Command Sponsored Dependent Travel Letter
<u>www.amc.af.mil/Portals/12/AMC%20Tvl%20Pg/Dual%20-%20Step%20Parent%20Auth%20Ltr%20(May%202018).pdf?ver=</u>[21]

Dual Parent/Step Parent Authorization Letter
<u>www.amc.af.mil/Portals/12/AMC%20Tvl%20Pg/Dual%20-%20Step%20Parent%20Auth%20Ltr%20(May%202018).pdf?ver=</u>[22]

30-Day & 365-Day Deployment Letter
<u>www.amc.af.mil/Portals/12/documents/AFD-160321-016.pdf</u>[23]
Spacea.net Space-A Forms, Sample Letters, and Documents
<u>www.spacea.net/regulations-forms-letters</u>[24]

Miscellaneous

Customs and Immigration Border Clearance

---

19.   http://www.amc.af.mil/Home/AMC-Travel-Site/AMC-Space-Available-Travel-Page/

20.   http://www.amc.af.mil/Portals/12/documents/

AFD-140922-057.pdf?ver=2016-05-18-115438-263

21.   http://www.amc.af.mil/Portals/12/AMC%20Tvl%20Pg/

Dual%20-%20Step%20Parent%20Auth%20Ltr%20(May%202018).pdf?ver=2018-05-15-1404

25-337

22.   http://www.amc.af.mil/Portals/12/AMC%20Tvl%20Pg/

Dual%20-%20Step%20Parent%20Auth%20Ltr%20(May%202018).pdf?ver=2018-05-15-1404

25-337

23.   http://www.amc.af.mil/Portals/12/documents/AFD-160321-016.pdf

24.   http://www.spacea.net/regulations-forms-letters

www.military.com/travel/space-available-flight-immigration-border-clearance.html[25]

U.S. Citizens Will Need to Register to Travel to Europe in 2021 www.etias.us/[26]

Sample AMCGRAM www.spaceaflights.net/amcgram_dover.pdf[27]

Officials break ground on hospital to replace Landstuhl www.stripes.com/news/officials-break-ground-on-hospital-to-replace-landstuhl-1.310376

25.   http://www.military.com/travel/space-available-flight-immigration-border-clearance.html

26.   http://www.etias.us/

27.   http://www.spaceaflights.net/amcgram_dover.pdf

Passenger Terminals with Social Media Pages

For those terminals that have a social media page, normally Facebook, you can post questions on their page and passenger terminal agents will attempt to answer your questions. Some terminals have discontinued posting to social media pages and now only post to official military websites.

AMC Stateside Social Media Pages

Baltimore-Washington IAP, Maryland
    Dover AFB, Delaware
    Fairchild AFB, Washington
    Jacksonville NAS, Florida
    JB Andrews, Maryland
    JB Charleston, South Carolina
    JB Lewis-McChord, Washington
    JB McGuire-Dix-Lakehurst, New Jersey
    Little Rock AFB, Arkansas
    MacDill AFB, Florida
    McConnell AFB, Kansas
    NS Norfolk, Virginia
    Pope Field, North Carolina
    Scott AFB, Illinois
    Seattle-Tacoma IAP, Washington
    Travis AFB, California

AMC Overseas Social Media Pages

Al Udeid AB, Qatar
    Andersen AB, Guam
    Aviano AB, Italy
    Eielson AFB, Alaska
    Incirlik AB, Turkey
    JB Elmendorf-Richardson, Alaska
    JB Pearl Harbor-Hickam, Hawaii
    Kadena AB, Okinawa, Japan
    Lajes AB, Azores, Portugal
    MCAS Iwakuni, Japan
    Misawa AB, Japan
    NAS Sigonella, Italy
    NS Guantanamo Bay, Cuba
    NS Rota, Spain
    NSA Bahrain, Bahrain
    NSA Naples, Italy
    NSA Souda Bay, Crete, Greece
    NSF Diego Garcia, British Indian Ocean
    Osan AB, Rep of Korea
    RAAF Base Richmond, Australia
    RAF Mildenhall, United Kingdom
    Ramstein AB, Germany
    Spangdahlem AB, Germany
    Yokota AB, Japan

Other Major Command Social Media Pages

Altus AFB (AETC), Oklahoma
    Beale AFB (ACC), California

Cannon AFB (AFSOC), New Mexico
Eglin AFB (AFMC), Florida
Hill AFB (AFMC), Utah
Holloman AFB (ACC), New Mexico
Hurlburt Field (AFSOC), Florida
JB San Antonio (AETC), Texas
Maxwell AFB (AETC), Alabama
MCAS Futenma (USMC), Okinawa, Japan
NAF Atsugi Air Terminal (USN), Japan
NAF North Island (USN), California
NAS Fort Worth JRB (USN), Texas
NAS Whidbey Island (USN), Washington
Nellis AFB (ACC), Nevada
Niagara Falls ARS (AFRC), New York
Patrick AFB (AFSPC), Florida
Peterson AFB (AFSPC), Colorado
Robins AFB (AFMC), Georgia
Seymour-Johnson AFB (ACC), North Carolina
Tinker AFB (AFMC), Oklahoma
Whiteman AFB (AFGSC), Missouri

Air National Guard Social Media Pages

101 ARW (ANG), Maine
103 AW (ANG), Connecticut
127 Wing (ANG), Selfridge ANGB, Michigan
133 AW (ANG), St Paul, Minnesota
137 ARW (ANG), Will Rogers World Airport, Oklahoma
145 AW (ANG), Charlotte, North Carolina
155 ARW Nebraska (ANG), Lincoln, Nebraska
157 ARW Pease ANGB (ANG), New Hampshire

161 ARW (ANG), Arizona
164 AW (ANG), Memphis, Tennessee
189 ARW (ANG), Sioux City, Iowa
190 ARW (ANG), Forbes Field, Kansas

Eligible Space-Available Travelers

Below are the official Space-A categories as well as the approved geographical travel segments per Table 3, *DoDI 4515.13*. The geographical travel segments list the origin and destination combinations. The segments pertain to CONUS and OCONUS. CONUS stands for Continental United States meaning the 48 contiguous states in the U.S. OCONUS stands for Outside the Continental United States meaning overseas including Hawaii and Alaska. If the geographical segment is not listed under a particular category segment, that means that travel is not authorized in that particular geographical segment. For example, "dependents of members of the uniformed services when accompanied by their sponsors and traveling in Category I status," which is shown below as #4, Category I, are authorized CONUS to CONUS but not OCONUS to OCONUS, CONUS to OCONUS or OCONUS to CONUS. For additional information see *DoDI 4515.13* or speak with a passenger terminal agent.

The segments are as follows:

C-C	CONUS to CONUS
O-O	OCONUS to OCONUS
C-O	CONUS to OCONUS
O-C	OCONUS to CONUS

The numbers within each category are a sequential numbering system for reference purposes only. They have no impact on the priority of travel within that category. For example, #1 and #4 in Category I are identical for priority purposes.

Category I - Emergency Leave Unfunded Travel.

Transportation by the most expeditious routing only for bona fide immediate family emergencies, as determined by *DoDI 1327.06* and Military Service regulations. This travel privilege will not be used in lieu of funded travel entitlements.

1. Wounded Warriors traveling on leave will be offered seats on Operational Support Airlift (OSA) aircraft on a space-available basis before any other potential space-available passenger.

C-C, O-O, C-O, O-C

2. Immediate family members of Wounded Warriors who possess a valid DoD identification card when accompanying Wounded Warriors to their destination on OSA aircraft.

C-C, O-O, C-O, O-C

3. Uniformed services members with emergency status indicated in leave orders.

C-C

4. Dependents of members of the uniformed services when accompanied by their sponsors and traveling in Category I status.

C-C

5. Unaccompanied dependents of members of the uniformed services who are assigned and domiciled in the CONUS.

C-O, O-C

6. Non command-sponsored dependents of members of the uniformed services, residing OCONUS with the sponsor; one-way only to emergency destination.

O-O, O-C

7. (1) Command-sponsored dependents of members of the uniformed Services; (2) DoD civilians and their command sponsored dependents; (3) American Red Cross (ARC) full-time, paid personnel serving with a DoD Component OCONUS; (4) Non-appropriated funds (NAF) personnel whose travel from the CONUS, Alaska, or Hawaii was incident to a PCS assignment at NAF expense.

O-O, C-O, O-C

8. Dependents of retired uniformed services members who die OCONUS are authorized travel from OCONUS to the CONUS, and OCONUS to OCONUS to accompany the remains of the deceased member. Return travel is authorized if accomplished within one year of arrival. The dependent will present documentation to air terminal personnel certified by DoD mortuary affairs offices. The documentation must be in the dependent's possession during travel.

O-O, C-O, O-C

Category II – Accompanied EML.

9. Sponsors in an EML status and their dependents traveling with them, also in an EML status. Sponsors include: (1)

uniformed services members; (2) U.S. citizen civilian employees of the Military Services who are eligible for government-funded transportation to the United States at tour completion (including NAF employees); (3) ARC fulltime, paid personnel on duty with a DoD Component OCONUS; (4) USO professional staff personnel on duty with the uniformed services; (5) DoD Education Activity teachers during the school year and during employer approved training during recess periods.

O-O, C-O, O-C

Category III - Ordinary Leave, Relatives, House Hunting Permissive TDY, Medal of Honor Holders, and Foreign Military.

10. Uniformed services members in ordinary leave or pass status.

C-C, O-O, C-O, O-C

11. Uniformed services members traveling under permissive TDY orders for house hunting incident to a pending PCS.

C-C, O-O, C-O, O-C

12. Relatives who are permanent members of the household and dependent upon a Military Service member, a DoD civilian employee, or an ARC employee serving with a DoD Component OCONUS, when the sponsor is authorized transportation of dependents at government expense. Travel must be in accordance with the sponsor or sponsor's dependents' PCS move.

O-O, C-O

13. Dependent spouses of military personnel officially reported in a missing status. Dependents and accompanying dependent children and parents, when traveling for humanitarian reasons and on approval on a case-by-case basis by the Chief of the Military Department or designated representative. Travelers will present approval document from the Service concerned.

C-C, O-O, C-O, O-C

14. Dependents of a uniformed services member when accompanied by their sponsor in ordinary leave or pass status.

C-C, O-O, C-O, O-C

15. Dependents when accompanying a uniformed services member traveling under permissive TDY orders for house hunting incident to a pending PCS.

C-C, O-O, C-O, O-C

16. Medal of Honor recipients and their accompanying dependents. Except for active duty, traveler will present a copy of the Medal of Honor award certificate or DD Form 2765 with designation "MH".

C-C, O-O, C-O, O-C

17. Command-sponsored dependents of uniformed services members accompanying their sponsors on approved circuitous travel. Commanders authorized to publish

circuitous travel orders for members under current policy of their uniformed service, where extenuating circumstances prevail, may approve requests for travel of their dependents within and between OCONUS areas and the CONUS incident to approved circuitous travel of the member.

O-O, C-O, O-C

18. Civilian U.S. Military Service patients who have recovered after treatment in medical facilities and their accompanying nonmedical attendants. Travel is permitted by the most expeditious routing to return the recovered patient and nonmedical attendant to their OCONUS post of assignment. (During the death or extended hospitalization of the patient, the nonmedical attendant retains the space-available travel authority to return to the patient's OCONUS post of assignment).

O-O, C-O

19. Foreign cadets and midshipmen attending U.S. Service academies in a leave status. Foreign cadets' and midshipmen's native countries must be identified in the leave authorization.

C-O, O-C

20. Foreign exchange service members on permanent duty with the DoD, when in a leave status.

C-C, O-O, C-O, O-C

21. Dependents of foreign exchange service members on permanent duty with the DoD, when accompanying their sponsors.

C-C, O-O, C-O, O-C

22. Unaccompanied dependents of deployed active duty uniformed services members when the deployment exceeds 365 consecutive days (passenger will be at the bottom of Category III).

C-C, O-O, C-O, O-C

23. Military personnel and civilian employees of the Ministry of Defence of the UK permanently assigned to Diego Garcia.

O-O

Category IV - Unaccompanied Environmental Morale Leave (EML).

24. Unaccompanied dependents traveling under the EML Program.

O-O, C-O, O-C

25. DoD Education Activity teachers and their dependents (accompanied or unaccompanied) traveling during the summer under the EML Program.

O-O, C-O, O-C

26. Unaccompanied dependents of deployed active duty uniformed services members when the deployment is for at least 30 consecutive days.

C-C, O-O, C-O, O-C

27. Uniformed services member retirees residing in commonwealths and U.S. possessions traveling to obtain certain health care services (medical or dental) and one dependent of the individual, if needed to accompany the individual.

O-O, C-O, O-C

28. Diego Garcia Third-Country Nationals (TCN) direct hire employees. Transportation is to and from the nearest intermediate destination serviced by commercial aircraft.

O-O

Category V - Permissive TDY (Non-House Hunting), Students, Dependents, Post Deployment/Mobilization Respite Absence, and Others.

29. Military personnel traveling on permissive TDY orders other than for house hunting.

C-C, O-O, C-O, O-C

30. Authorized dependents who are in-residence college students attending an OCONUS branch of an American (i.e., U.S.) university located in the same OCONUS area in which they reside, command-sponsored, stationed

OCONUS with their sponsor, who is: (1) a member of the uniformed services; (2) a U.S. citizen civilian employee of the DoD (paid from either appropriated funds or NAF); or (3) an ARC full-time, paid employee serving with the DoD. Unaccompanied travel is permitted from the OCONUS military passenger terminal nearest the sponsor's permanent duty station (PDS) to the OCONUS military passenger terminal nearest the university during school breaks. Return travel is authorized. Students must present written authorization from the sponsor's approving authority. Only one round trip each year is authorized and unused trips may not be accumulated from school year to school year.

O-O

31.   Dependents, command-sponsored, stationed OCONUS with their sponsor, who is: (1) a uniformed services member; (2) a U.S. citizen civilian employee of the DoD (paid from either appropriated funds or NAF); or (3) an ARC full-time, paid employee serving with the DoD. Unaccompanied travel is permitted to and from the nearest OCONUS military academy testing site to take scheduled entrance examinations for entry into any of the U.S. Military Service Academies.

O-O

32. Dependents of active duty U.S. military personnel stationed OCONUS who, at the time of PCS, were not entitled to transportation at government expense. Travel is to accompany or join their sponsor at his or her duty station. Travel may be unaccompanied and is limited to travel from the aerial port of embarkation (APOE) in the CONUS,

Alaska, or Hawaii to the OCONUS aerial port of debarkation (APOD) serving the sponsor's duty station.

C-O

33. Non-command sponsored dependents, acquired in an OCONUS area during a military member's current tour of assigned duty, not otherwise entitled to transportation at government expense. Command regulations pertaining to the acquisition of dependents must be followed. Travel must be with the member's PCS, may be unaccompanied, and is limited to travel from the OCONUS APOE to the APOD in the CONUS, Alaska, or Hawaii. Member's PCS orders are required for travel.

O-C

34. Unaccompanied spouses of uniformed services members stationed in OCONUS areas in response to written requests from school officials or when deemed essential, authorized, and directed in writing by the sponsor's commander for personal consultation on matters about the needs of dependent members attending school at an OCONUS location away from the uniformed services member's PDS.

O-O

35. Command-sponsored dependents of uniformed services members, unaccompanied, who are stationed OCONUS. Travel restrictions may apply to certain OCONUS destinations as determined by the combatant commander (CCDR). Documentation signed by the sponsor's commander verifying command sponsorship will be presented to air terminal personnel, and be in the

dependent's possession during travel. Dependents under 18 years of age must be accompanied by an eligible parent or legal guardian.

O-O, C-O, O-C

36. Non-command sponsored dependents of Active Duty personnel on a remote PCS tour. Approval must be granted in advance by the member's commander. A copy of the written approval must be presented to the air terminal personnel.

O-O, C-O, O-C

37. Service members and their dependents traveling on post deployment/mobilization respite absence.

C-C, O-O, C-O, O-C

Category VI – Retired, Dependents, Reserve, ROTC, NUPOC, CEC members, and Veterans with a Permanent Service-connected Disability Rated as Total.

38. Retired uniformed services members.

C-C, O-O, C-O, O-C

39. Dependents of retired uniformed services members when accompanying their sponsors.

C-C, O-O, C-O, O-C

40.   Dependents, command-sponsored, stationed OCONUS with their sponsor, who is: (1) a uniformed services member; (2) a U.S. citizen civilian employee of the DoD (paid from either appropriated funds or NAF); or (3) an ARC full-time, paid employee serving with the DoD. Unaccompanied travel is permitted to the United States for enlisting in one of the Military Services when local enlistment in the OCONUS area is not authorized. If an applicant for military service is rejected, return travel to the OCONUS area may be provided under this eligibility.

O-O, C-O, O-C

41. Authorized Reserve Component (RC) members and authorized RC members entitled to retired pay at age 60 (i.e., "gray area retirees") traveling in the CONUS or directly between the CONUS and Alaska, Hawaii, Puerto Rico, the U.S. Virgin Islands, Guam, and American Samoa (Guam and American Samoa travelers may transit Hawaii or Alaska); or traveling within Alaska, Hawaii, Puerto Rico or the U.S. Virgin Islands.

C-C

42. NUPOC, CEC, and ROTC students of the Army, Navy, or Air Force receiving financial assistance or enrolled in advanced training, in uniform, during authorized absences from the school. Travel is authorized within and between the CONUS, Alaska, Hawaii, and the U.S. territories.

C-C

43. Newly-commissioned ROTC officers who are awaiting the call to extended active duty. Travel is authorized within and between the CONUS, Alaska, Hawaii, and the U.S. territories.

C-C

44. American Samoa veterans residing in America Samoa traveling to and from Hawaii for hospital care from the VA facility in Hawaii. To and from Hawaii only. Dependent who accompanied a Service member while the Service member obtained health care services and subsequently died.

O-O, C-O, O-C

45. Employees of the ARC, USO, and USS when providing direct support to the U.S. Military Services.

C-O, O-C

46. Special Category Residents (Cuban exiles)

To and from Cuba only

47. Individuals at Guantanamo Bay, Cuba, as identified in Section 4.8.p. of this issuance. Such passengers will be at the bottom of the Category VI sign-up register.

To and from and Cuba only

48. Authorized veterans with a permanent service-connected disability rated as total traveling in the CONUS or directly between the CONUS and Alaska, Hawaii, Puerto Rico, the U.S. Virgin Islands, Guam, and

American Samoa (Guam and American Samoa travelers may transit Hawaii or Alaska); or traveling within Alaska, Hawaii, Puerto Rico, or the U.S. Virgin Islands.

C-C

Time Zones

The world is divided into 24 time zones or areas. The zero-time zone is known as Greenwich Mean Time (GMT), also referred to as Zulu Time, which is physically located in Greenwich, England (UK), near London. Other areas in this time zone include Iceland, Ascension Island, England, Scotland, and Portugal. Local conditions such as Daylight Savings Time, may alter the exact time of a particular zone or area. Below are some of the time zones in the world.

Pago Pago, AS -11
Hawaii -10
Elmendorf, AK -9
Pacific Time U.S. -8
Mountain Time U.S. -7
Central Time U.S. -6
Eastern Time U.S. -5
Bermuda/Chile/Puerto Rico -4
Azores, PO -1
Ascension/England/Portugal GMT
Germany/Italy/Spain +1
Egypt/Greece/Israel/Turkey +2
Bahrain +3
Oman/United Arab Emirates +4
Diego Garcia/Kyrgyzstan +5
Jakarta, Singapore/Thailand +7
Philippines/Taiwan +8
Japan/Korea/Palau +9
Alice Springs, (AU) +9:30
Guam/Richmond (AU) +10
Kwajalein Atoll/New Zealand +12

In order to determine the particular time of another location, calculate the difference between your local time and the other location using the chart above.

For example, you are in Hawaii and it is 11am and you want to know the time in Germany. Per the chart above, Hawaii is at -10 and Germany is at +1. The difference between the two time zones is 11 (there are 11 time zones between the two locations), so you would add 11 to 11am which is 10pm. The time in Germany is 10pm when it is 11am in Hawaii.

Most cell phones have a World Clock or similar feature that help in determining time zones without the need for math.

Twenty-Four Hour Clock/Military Time

Military time is calculated using 24 hours. Between midnight and noon, military time is the same as conventional clock time (0100 = 1am, 0900 = 9am) but between noon and midnight, you will need to add "12" to the time to convert from conventional clock time to military time (2pm = 1400, 8pm = 2000). The table below illustrates the differences.

Conventional Clock Military Clock
    Midnight 12am 2400 hours
    1am 0100 hours
    2am 0200 hours
    3am 0300 hours
    4am 0400 hours
    5am 0500 hours
    6am 0600 hours
    7am 0700 hours
    8am 0800 hours
    9am 0900 hours
    10am 1000 hours
    11am 1100 hours

Noon 12pm 1200 hours

1pm 1300 hours

2pm 1400 hours

3pm 1500 hours

4pm 1600 hours

5pm 1700 hours

6pm 1800 hours

7pm 1900 hours

8pm 2000 hours

9pm 2100 hours

10pm 2200 hours

11pm 2300 hours

Most cell phones will let you switch between the conventional clock format and military time.

Abbreviations

Acronyms

AAF - Army Airfield

AAFES - Army Air Force Exchange System

AD - Active Duty

ADT - Active Duty for Training

AE - Army Europe

AF - Air Force

AFAF - Air Force Auxiliary Field

AFB - Air Force Base

AFRC - Armed Forces Reserve Center or Armed Forces Recreation Center

AFRES - Air Force Reserve

AFS - Air Force Station

AGS - Air Guard Station

AIRVAC - Air Evacuation

AMC - Air Mobility Command or Army Medical Center

AMCI – Air Mobility Command Instruction

ANG - Air National Guard

ANGB - Air National Guard Base

AP - Army Pacific

APG - Army Proving Ground

APO - Army Post Office

APS - Army Port Squadron

ARB - Air Reserve Base

ARC – American Red Cross

ARNGB - Army National Guard Base

ARS - Air Reserve Station

ARW - Air Refueling Wing

AS - Air Station

AST - Area Support Team

ATC - Air Traffic Control

ATM - Automatic Teller Machine

AUX - Auxiliary

AW - Air Wing

BAQ - Bachelor Airmen's Quarters

BEQ - Bachelor Enlisted Quarters

BOH - Bachelor Officers' Housing

BOQ - Bachelor Officers Quarters

BQ - Bachelor Quarters

BRAC - Base Realignment and Closure

BSB - Base Support Battalion

BX - Base Exchange

C - Commercial Telephone System

CATV - Cable Television

CBH - Combined Bachelors Housing

CBQ - Combined Bachelors Quarters

CG - Coast Guard

CGAS - Coast Guard Air Station

CGES - Coast Guard Exchange System

CGISC - Coast Guard Integrated Support

CGSC - Coast Guard Support Center

CGTC - Coast Guard Training Center

CMD - Command

CMSgt - Chief Master Sergeant

CO - Commanding Officer

CONUS - Continental United States

CPO - Chief Petty Officer

CPOQ - Chief Petty Officer Quarters

CSM - Command Sergeant Major

CWO - Chief Warrant Officer

DAV - Disabled American Veterans

DGQ - Distinguished Guest Quarters
DHS - Department of Homeland Security
DoD - Department of Defense
DoDEA – Department of Defense Education Activity
DoT - Department of Transportation
DSN - Defense Switched Network
DTG – Date Time Group
DV - Distinguished Visitor
DVOQ - Distinguished Visiting Officers' Quarters
DVQ - Distinguished Visitor Quarters
EFQ - Enlisted Family Quarters
EM - Enlisted Members
EML - Environmental & Morale Leave
EMTG - European Military Travel Guide
FAMCAMP - Family Campground
FBO – Fixed Base Operator
FCU - Federal Credit Union
FIS - Federal Inspection Services
FPO - Fleet Post Office
FSS - Force Support Squadron
FW - Fighter Wing
GAFB - Greek Air Force Base
GMT - Greenwich Mean Time
GS - General Schedule
HOP – Slang for Space-A Flight
IAP - International Airport
IATA - International Air Transport Association
ICAO - International Civil Aviation Organization
ITR - Information, Ticketing and Registration
ITT - Information, Ticket and Tours
JFTB - Joint Forces Training Base
JRB - Joint Reserve Base

LI - Location Identifier
LPR - Legal Permanent Residents
LRS - Logistics Readiness Squadron
LST - Local Standard Time
MAC – Military Air Command (Replaced by AMC)
MCAF - Marine Corps Air Facility
MCAS - Marine Corps Air Station
MCB - Marine Corps Base
MCCS - Marine Corps Community Services
MCLB - Marine Corps Logistics Base
MCPO - Master Chief Petty Officer
MCRD - Marine Corps Recruit Depot
MCX - Marine Corps Exchange
MEDEVAC - Aeromedical Evacuation
MP - Military Police
MWR - Morale, Welfare and Recreation
NAB - Naval Amphibious Base
NAES - Naval Air Engineering Station
NAF - Naval Air Facility
NAF - Non - appropriated Funds
NALF - Naval Auxiliary Landing Field
NARS - Naval Air Reserve Station
NAS - Naval Air Station
NASA - National Aeronautics & Space Administration
NATO - North Atlantic Treaty Organization
NAVAIR - Naval Air Systems Command
NAWC - Naval Air Warfare Center
NAWS - Naval Air Weapons Station
NCBC - Naval Construction Battalion Center
NCO - Non - commissioned Officer
NEX - Navy Exchange
NFCU - Navy Federal Credit Union

NG - National Guard
NNMC - National Naval Medical Center
NOAA - National Oceanic & Atmospheric Administration
NS - Naval Station
NSA - Naval Support Activity
NSB - Naval Submarine Base
NSCS - Naval Supply Corps School
NSGA - Naval Security Group Activity
NSWC - Naval Surface Warfare Center
NSYD - Naval Shipyard
NTC - National Training Center or NTC - Naval Training Center
NTTC - Naval Technical Training Center
NWC - Naval Weapons Center
OAFB - Oman Air Force Base
O Club - Officers' Club
OCONUS - Outside Continental United
OIC - Officer in Charge
OOD - Officer of the Day
OSA – Operational Support Airlift
PAC - Pacific
PAO - Public Affairs Officer
PAT - Patriot Express
PAX - Passenger
PCS - Permanent Change of Station
PE - Patriot Express
PG - Proving Ground
PHS - Public Health Service
PMO - Provost Marshall's Office
POV - Privately Owned Vehicle
PMRF - Pacific Missile Range Facility
PSA - Passenger Service Representative
PX - Post Exchange

RAAFB - Royal Australian Air Force Base
RAF - Royal Air Force
RAFB - Royal Air Force Base
ROKAB - Republic of Korea Air Base
RON - Remain Over Night
RSAF - Royal Singapore Air Force
RV - Recreational Vehicle
RVC - Recreational Vehicle Center
SARPS - Standard and Recommended Practices
SATV - Satellite Television
SDO - Staff Duty Officer
SES - Senior Executive Service
SHAPE - Supreme Headquarters Allied Powers Europe
SNCO - Senior Non - commissioned Officer
SNCOQ - Senior Noncommissioned Officers' Quarters
SOFA - Status of Forces Agreement
SOQ - Senior Officers' Quarters
SP - Security Police
Space-A - Space Available
TAD - Temporary Attached Duty
TAQ - Temporary Airmen's Quarters
TCH - Trans - Canada Highway
TDY - Temporary Duty
TEQ - Temporary Enlisted Quarters
TFQ - Temporary Family Quarters
TLA - Temporary Lodging Allowance
TLF - Transient Lodging Facility
TLQ - Temporary Living Quarters
TML - Temporary Military Lodging
TRANS - Transportation Squadron
TOQ - Transient Officers' Quarters
TQ - Temporary Quarters

TSQ - Transient Staff NCO Quarters
TVEQ - Temporary Visiting Enlisted Quarters
TVOQ - Temporary Visiting Officers' Quarters
TVQ - Temporary Visiting Quarters
UPH - Unaccompanied Personnel Housing
USA - United States Army
USAF - United States Air Force
USCG - United States Coast Guard
USDAO - United States Defense Attaché Office
USEUCOM - United States European Command
USMC - United States Marine Corps
USMLO - United States Military Liaison Office
USMRA - United States Military Road Atlas
USN - United States Navy
USPS - United States Postal Service
USO - United Service Organization
USPHS - United States Public Health Service
VA - Veterans' Administration
VAQ - Visiting Airmen's Quarters
VAT - Value Added Tax
VEQ - Visiting Enlisted Quarters
VFQ - Visiting Female Quarters
VHA - Variable Housing Allowance
VIP - Very Important Person
VOQ - Visiting Officer Quarters
VQ - Visiting Quarters, All Ranks
VWP - Visa Waiver Program
WO - Warrant Officer
ZULU - Common Time Zone

About the Author

Marcus and his family utilized Space-A to inexpensively travel around the world. Space-A travel truly added an element of adventure into yearly family vacations. Now that their children are grown, Marcus and his wife Sheila expect to continue to use this resource to further expand their travels. They currently reside in Monterey, California.